JOSEPHI[NE]
CHEESECAKES

HAMLYN

First published in 1986 by
Hamlyn Publishing
Bridge House, London Road,
Twickenham, Middlesex, England

Copyright © Hamlyn Publishing, a division of
The Hamlyn Publishing Group Limited

Produced by New Leaf Productions

Photography by Mick Duff
Design by Jim Wire
Typeset by System Graphics Ltd, Folkestone
Series Editor: James M. Gibson

ISBN 0 600 32639 X

Printed in Spain   Lito. A. Romero, S. A. – D. L. TF. 813 – 1986

NOTE
1. Metric and imperial measurements have been
   calculated separately. Use one set of measurements
   only as they are not exact equivalents.
2. All spoon measures are level unless otherwise
   stated.

We would like to thank:
Vanessa Vasey and Kate Evelyn Hackman for their
help and use of their kitchens. Jean Jackson of Los
Angeles, U.S.A. and Bruce Johnson of Copenhagen,
Denmark, for their assistance. All cheeses, yogurt,
soured cream and cream for testing these recipes have
been supplied by Raines Dairies, Enfield, Middlesex.
also:
Nasons of Canterbury for the loan of crockery,
tablecloths, napkins, etc.

Home economy/food styling by Nichola Palmer

CONTENTS

INTRODUCTION

Cheesecakes are among the oldest cakes known to mankind. As soon as the secret of cheesemaking was discovered, fresh curds were sweetened and eaten raw or, more likely, cooked, since they deteriorated quickly. We know that the ancient Egyptians made curds and ate them sweetened. Demosthenes, Aristophanes and Socrates all extolled the glories of cakes made with curds and honey. Cato even has a recipe for cheesecake made with honey, eggs and poppyseeds, which I have tried to reproduce in this book (see page 20).

Almost every country has its own versions of the cheesecake. Sweet cheese cakes are mostly made with the soft, unmatured cheeses (curd, cottage or cream cheeses), some even use strongly flavoured cheeses such as Cheddar and Edam. Oddly enough, it seems as though the only country which does not have sweet cheesecakes in its repertory of national dishes is France.

In Britain, cheesecakes seem to have been confined to the Midlands, Yorkshire and the Northeast. In spite of the large sheep population, they seem always to have been made from cow's milk. Although there are many local recipes, the type of cheesecake which has become most popular in Britain is actually an import from central Europe.

This book gives recipes for the most popular cheesecakes, as well as introducing the reader to different types of cheesecake from all over the world, from Albania to the Philippines. Some of these cakes can be whipped up in a matter of minutes (especially if you have a microwave oven); others are special occasion cakes that require longer preparation. There are also recipes for cheese pies, tarts, flans, a few savoury cheesecake recipes and even cheesecakes without cheese!

Soft cheeses for cheesecakes

Most cheesecakes are made with soft cheeses. These are freshly made cheeses which have not been allowed to mature. They dry up and go mouldy very quickly; thus they should always be bought as close as possible to the time they are to be used.

Cream cheese is often specified as a cheesecake ingredient. True cream cheese is not usually available because it does not keep well, since it is not really a cheese, simply cream which has drained and set.

Full-fat soft cheeses described in the shops as cream cheeses can have a butter fat content of over 65%. These are also unsuitable for baked cheesecakes, as they can become grainy or separate during cooking. They will also separate if frozen. When a cheesecake recipe specifies cream cheese as an ingredient, use a full-fat soft cheese with less than 65% fat content.

The fat content is always stated on the packaging. By law, any cheese labelled "full-fat soft cheese" must have a butterfat content of at least 20%. Medium-fat soft cheese contains 10–20% fat; use it where the recipe calls for curd cheese, or use cheese with a low fat content.

Cottage cheese, a very popular cheesecake ingredient, is the simplest cheese to make and has a low- to medium-fat content. The specific amount of fat in cottage cheese is not important, since there is no such thing as full-fat cottage cheese. However, the cheeses with a higher fat content have a better flavour. There are also soft, fresh cheeses made from whey. The best-known and most widely available in Britain are the Italian Ricotta and the Greek Mizithra, known in Cyprus as Anari (with the accent on the "i") or in Turkish as Noor. These cheeses are made in wicker baskets which leave the pattern of their twigs on the outsides. They are traditionally made from ewes' milk, but nowadays are more often produced from cows' milk. Supermarkets stock a wide variety of full-fat, medium-fat, and low-fat soft cheeses, as well as cottage cheeses. The fresh whey cheeses are usually available only from speciality shops, though the better supermarkets will stock them.

Philadelphia is a full-fat soft cheese which is stabilized by the addition of carob gum. It is the most frequently used cheese in American cheesecakes. In this book, the brand name Philadelphia is specified, in order to make the meaning clear. However, some books refer to it as "processed cream cheese".

Quark is a German and Austrian very smooth white cheese. Plain Quark is sometimes slightly flavoured with vanilla, making it ideal for sweet desserts. The fat content can be low or medium.

Soured cream and crème fraîche

When soured cream is specified in recipes, the reference is to commercially cultured soured cream. Recently, the milder, slightly sour, French crème fraîche has become more easily available in this country, and it can be used instead. The flavour is milder than that of soured cream. Crème fraîche can be simulated by mixing 1 tablespoon buttermilk into 600 ml/1 pint of whipping cream, and leaving the mixture in a warm place for 2-3 hours. Another substitute for soured cream is thick Greek yogurt. Other kinds of natural yogurt are too thin to be suitable substitutes if the recipe specifies soured cream. Soured cream can also be made at home by adding 2 teaspoons lemon juice to 250 ml/8 fl oz evaporated milk.

Making your own cheese for cheesecakes

It is fun to make your own cheeses for cheesecake. Cheese is easiest to make from natural yogurt, since natural yogurt already contains the microbe that curdles cheese. If made from milk, it is best made from raw (unpasteurized) milk. However, it can be made from pasteurized milk, but do not use UHT or long-life milk. In addition to milk or natural yogurt and rennet, to curdle the cheese, you will need two large bowls and cheesecloth, a large square of unstarched muslin such as is used for bandages. Boil the cloth before use to sterilise it. If the cheesemaking instructions conflict with the manufacturer's instructions for the rennet, the latter should be followed. Always use home-made cheeses within 48 hours of making.

LOW-FAT CHEESE MADE FROM NATURAL YOGURT
Makes 450 g/1 lb

This cheese can be used where either low-fat or cottage cheese is specified.

2.25 litres/4 pints natural yogurt

Line a sieve or colander with cheesecloth and suspend it over a deep bowl. Pour the natural yogurt into the cheesecloth. Let it drain for 8 hours or overnight. Refrigerate and use as soon as possible.

CURD CHEESE FROM MILK
Makes 450 g/1 lb

2.25 litres/4 pints skimmed milk
1 teaspoon rennet

Make the milk into a junket according to the rennet manufacturer's instructions. Arrange two layers of cheesecloth over a large sieve suspended over a large bowl. Tip the junket into the cheesecloth, scraping down the sides. Draw up the corners of the cheesecloth to form a bag and tie it firmly closed. Hang it up to drain for 8 hours or overnight. Open the bag in the sieve, scrape down the sides and hang up for a further 8 hours. Repeat the procedure and leave for 24 hours. The cheese should now be suitable for use in cakes. For full-fat soft cheese, use full-cream or whole milk and follow the same procedure.

HOME-MADE COTTAGE CHEESE
Makes 450 g/1 lb

2.25 litres/4 pints skimmed milk
4 tablespoons buttermilk or natural yogurt

Combine the skimmed milk and buttermilk or natural yogurt. Leave them, covered, in a bowl for 24 hours in a warm place. Warm the milk to blood heat (test it with your finger), to separate the curd from the whey. Strain the curd into a cheesecloth laid over a sieve. Drain it, scraping the curd down from the sides to the centre. Tie up the bag and hang it for 8 hours or until the cheese is firm enough to use.

CLASSIC CHEESECAKES

The type of cheesecake with which we are all now familiar and to which I refer in this book as the classic cheesecake was, surprisingly, almost unknown in Britain before World War II. In fact, it is an import from Germany and Austria, and was introduced by refugees. At first, it could only be bought from Jewish and continental bakers; nowadays, it is as familiar a sight at the corner café as Dundee cake and Bakewell tart. There are even "instant" cheesecake mixes, but they are not nearly as delicious (or healthy) as truly home-made cheesecake.

Classic or continental cheesecakes consist of a firm, thin base, often made from crushed biscuits or cake, a fluffy or creamy filling made with soft, white cheese, and sometimes a topping. There are two kinds of classic cheesecake, baked and unbaked. For both, the fillings need to be very smoothly blended. Electric beaters are best for this task.

The base for classic cheesecakes

The base for most cheesecakes consists of a pre-cooked biscuit or cake which is crushed and mixed with butter or chocolate; sometimes a flavouring such as cinnamon is added. Sometimes these crumb bases are baked blind before the topping is added. Some cheesecakes have pastry bases, and these are sometimes prebaked and sometimes not. Prebaking will made the base crisper and less porous. If pastry bases for baked cheesecakes are not prebaked, they must be made of ingredients which will prevent the fillings from seeping through them during chilling or baking. Prebaked sponge bases are also used occasionally for unbaked cheesecakes. However, most bases are made from crushed biscuits or crumbled sponge cakes.

The easiest way to crush or crumble biscuits or cakes is to put them into a food processor and grind them with the metal blade. A blender can also be used for crushing, but will only crush small quantities at a time. Make sure all the equipment for crushing is completely dry, or you will end up with a soggy paste. The base must completely cover the bottom of the tin (sometimes it extends up the sides) to stop the filling from leaking out.

To crush biscuits or cakes without electrical equipment, put them into a strong polythene bag. Squeeze the bag to remove the air, then crush the biscuits with a rolling pin. Another way is to crush the biscuits or cakes in a large bowl, using a rolling pin with flat ends, a jam jar, or a heavy weight.

Tins for baking classic cheesecakes

Cheesecake differs from all other cakes in that the pan cannot be upended to remove the cake, since the cake is too fragile, especially when warm. For this reason, classic cheesecakes are normally baked in a tin from which they can be removed right way up without difficulty. The best tin for the purpose is a springform tin, a tin with a removable base and sides which expand when the clip which holds them together is released. Other loose-bottomed tins without expanding sides can also be used. These tins are available from cookware shops, from better iron-mongers and from well-stocked cookery departments of big stores. It is best to use shiny tins, as they reflect the heat and will prevent the cheesecakes from burning. The sides of the tins should be lightly greased. Cheap, disposable foil tins with loose bottoms and about half the capacity of a standard springform tin are now obtainable. You can also use a conventional cake tin and line it with foil. Leave enough foil overlapping the edge (fold it down over the outside edges) so that you can use it to lift the cake out of the tin when cooked.

Baking the classic cheesecake

Cheesecakes need slow baking, to prevent cracking and sinking. Some cracking will always occur, and sinking can be disguised with judicious use of toppings. To prevent sinking while a cheesecake cools after baking, turn the oven off and leave the cake in the oven with the door ajar for 1 hour, then cool the cake in the tin for a further hour before chilling it. To remove a cheesecake easily from springform or loose-bottomed tin, place the cake on top of a tall tin, such as a big coffee tin or upturned flowerpot. When the spring is released, the sides can drop downwards.

Cheesecakes in the microwave oven

Baked classic cheesecakes can be successfully cooked in a microwave oven. In fact, if you suspect your conventional oven does not distribute the heat very evenly, you may find a microwave oven produces better results.

Use a microwave cake dish, first lining it with cling film. Wrap excess cling film over the outer sides. When the cake is baked, let it cool in the dish as you would a conventionally baked cheesecake, then use the cling film to lift it out. A cheesecake will cook in 12 minutes on medium in a 700 watt oven. If you do not have a turntable, the cake must be turned a quarter turn every three minutes. Do not use a microwave oven for other types of cheesecake in this book, unless the instructions specifically call for it.

Glazes and toppings for the classic cheesecake
The classic cheesecake can be glazed or spread with fruit or other topping. Do *not* unmould the cheesecake before glazing or topping it, unless you specifically want the topping to drip down the sides of the cake.

The best jellies for glazing are the quick-setting varieties in powder form that contain carageen or agar or the quick-setting jelly specially made for glazing cakes. Any kind of jam or marmalade can be used as a topping. Warm it by standing the jar in a saucepan of water to come two-thirds up the sides of the jar. Spread it on with a palette knife while the cake is still in its tin.

One of the most popular cheesecake toppings, due to the attractive colour contrast, is blackcurrant topping. Blackcurrant liqueur can be added, if desired.

BLACKCURRANT TOPPING
Enough to top a 23-cm/9-inch cake

300-g/10½-oz can blackcurrants in syrup
1 tablespoon arrowroot, cornflour or potato flour

Strain the blackcurrants through a sieve. Pour the syrup into a saucepan and heat gently. Mix the cornflour with 2 tablespoons water and stir this into the syrup. Bring to the boil, stirring. Add the blackcurrants and remove from the heat. Let cool to lukewarm before spreading on the cooled cake.

BAKED CLASSIC CHEESECAKES

CREAMY CHEESECAKE
Serves 10

This is a light cheesecake with mild flavouring. This makes it suitable for adding toppings, a few of which are suggested on page 7. There is no need to add a topping, however, for this cake tastes good without.

For the base
225 g/8 oz digestive biscuits, crushed
½ teaspoon ground cinnamon
75 g/3 oz butter, melted

For the filling
4 eggs, separated
225 g/8 oz sugar
250 ml/8 fl oz soured cream
½ teaspoon vanilla essence
2 tablespoons flour
450 g/1 lb full-fat soft cheese
icing sugar for dredging

To make the base, combine the crushed biscuits, butter, and cinnamon and spread them evenly over the base and 1 cm/½ inch up the sides of a lightly greased 23-cm/9-inch springform or loose-bottomed tin. Refrigerate until required.

Beat the egg yolks with 175 g/6 oz of the sugar until pale-coloured. Add the soured cream, vanilla and flour, beating until the mixture is smooth. Gradually beat in the cheese. Whisk the egg whites into soft peaks, then gradually beat in the rest of the sugar. Fold this meringue into the mixture. Pour the mixture into the tin. Bake in a preheated moderate oven (180°C, 350°F, Gas 4) for 1 hour. Let cool, then chill. Dredge with icing sugar just before serving.

QUICK AND EASY FRUIT-TOPPED CHEESECAKE

Serves 10 to 12

If you cannot get Ricotta or Mizithra cheese, drain enough cottage cheese (leave it in a sieve over a bowl for 30 minutes) to make up the correct quantity.

For the base
225-g/8-oz packet crumble topping
½ teaspoon ground cinnamon
4 tablespoons melted butter

For the filling
450 g/1 lb Ricotta, Mizithra *or* drained cottage cheese
450-g/1-lb tub natural yogurt
4 drops vanilla essence
1 teaspoon lemon juice
1 teaspoon grated lemon rind
3 eggs
225 g/8 oz sugar
4 tablespoons flour

For the topping
400-g/14-oz can blackcurrant *or* redcurrant and raspberry pie filling

To make the base, combine the crumble topping, cinnamon and butter, and spread the mixture over the base and up the sides of a 20-cm/8-inch diameter cake tin, pressing it down well with the back of a spoon. Bake the base in a preheated moderate oven (180°C, 350°F, Gas 4) for 10 minutes while you make the filling.

To make the filling, thoroughly mix the ingredients in the order given. Pour the mixture into the tin and bake in a preheated moderate oven (180°C, 350°F, Gas 4) for 1 hour. Cool and chill. Then spread on the topping.

PHILADELPHIA CHEESECAKE
Serves 12

This is another mild-flavoured cheesecake ideal for topping, when cold, with fruit, glaze or jelly.

For the base
225 g/8 oz Marie or other semi-sweet biscuits, crushed
3 tablespoons caster sugar
3 tablespoons melted butter

For the filling
450 g/1 lb Philadelphia cream cheese, at room temperature
100 g/4 oz caster sugar
2 tablespoons flour
¼ teaspoon salt
4 eggs, separated
175 ml/6 fl oz double cream
½ teaspoon vanilla essence
½ teaspoon lemon essence

For the topping
425-g/15-oz can mandarin orange segments, drained
1 packet orange-flavoured quick setting jelly

Make the base by combining, the ingredients and pressing them onto the bottom of a 23-cm/9-inch springform tin. Bake the base in a preheated moderate oven (160°C, 325°F, Gas 3) for 10 minutes.

To make the filling, beat the cheese until it is fluffy. Beat in the sugar, flour, and salt until smoothly blended. Beat in the egg yolks, one at a time, beating well after each addition. Then beat in the cream and flavouring essences. Whisk the egg whites into stiff peaks and fold them into the mixture. Pour the filling into the tin and bake it in a moderate oven (160°C, 325°F, Gas 3) for 1 hour. Cool and chill.

Arrange mandarin segments on top of the cheesecake. Make up the jelly following the directions on the packet and spoon over the mandarins. Chill until set.

CALIFORNIA WALNUT CHEESECAKE
Serves 10

This tasty cheesecake has less fat than some other cheesecakes. Since there is no base to the cake, the tin needs to be lined.

450 g/1 lb low-fat curd or cottage cheese
100 g/4 oz demerara sugar
3 eggs, beaten
2 tablespoons flour
100 g/4 oz chopped walnuts
10 walnut halves, to decorate

Beat the cheese, sugar, eggs and flour until smooth. Stir in the chopped walnuts and mix well. Line the base and sides of a 23-cm/9-inch springform or loose-bottomed cake tin with greased greaseproof baking paper. Pour the mixture into the tin and bake it in a preheated moderate oven (180°C, 350°F, Gas 4) for 50 minutes. Cool before removing from the tin. Decorate with walnuts.

SOURED CREAM CHEESECAKE
Serves 12

This cake has a baked soured cream topping which goes particularly well with a fresh fruit topping, added after baking. Use fresh berries, sliced apples, bananas (sprinkled with lemon juice to prevent browning) or mangoes, in fact, any fruit except fresh pineapple (see note under Pineapple Cheesecake, page 14).

For the base
225 g/8 oz ginger biscuits, crushed
½ teaspoon ground cinnamon
½ teaspoon ground allspice
75 g/3 oz butter, melted

For the filling
450 g/1 lb full-fat soft cheese, at room temperature
100 g/4 oz caster sugar
rind and juice of 1 lemon
½ teaspoon vanilla essence
2 eggs, separated

For the topping
250 ml/8 fl oz soured cream
2 tablespoons sugar
1 teaspoon vanilla essence

Decoration
50 g/2 oz ginger biscuits, crushed
2 bananas, sliced
lemon juice

Combine the ingredients for the base and spread them evenly over the base and 1 cm/½ inch up the sides of a lightly greased 23-cm/9-inch springform or loose-bottomed tin. Bake the base in a preheated moderate oven (160°C, 325°F, Gas 3) oven for 10 minutes.

Beat the cheese until fluffy. Beat in the sugar, lemon rind, lemon juice and vanilla essence until the mixture is smooth. Add the egg yolks, one by one, beating well after each addition. Whisk the egg whites until they are stiff. Fold them into the mixture. Bake the cake in a preheated moderate oven (160°C, 325°F, Gas 3) for 45 minutes. Remove the cake from the oven.

Beat the topping ingredients until smooth. Pour them over the cake and return it to the oven. Bake the cake for a further 10 minutes. Cool, then chill.

Arrange a border of crushed ginger biscuits around the top of the cheesecake. Dip the banana slices into the lemon juice and arrange in the centre.

LINDY'S CHEESECAKE
Serves 10

American cheesecakes are notoriously rich and sinful. The archetypal American cheesecake comes from Lindy's famous restaurants in New York City (one branch is in the Empire State Building). It is so good that it is sent all over the world to well-known people who cannot live without it. It has become immortalised in literature in the stories of Damon Runyan (though he disguised it under the name "Mindy's"). The official recipe is a closely guarded secret, but here is an approximate re-creation.

For the base
100 g/4 oz self-raising flour
50 g/2 oz icing sugar, sifted
1 teaspoon grated lemon rind
¼ teaspoon vanilla essence
1 egg yolk
65 g/2½ oz butter, softened

For the filling
900 g/2 lb curd cheese, at room temperature
225 g/8 oz low-fat soft cheese, at room temperature
225 g/8 oz caster sugar
2 tablespoons flour
2 teaspoons grated orange rind
2 teaspoons grated lemon rind
1 teaspoon lemon juice
½ teaspoon vanilla essence
5 eggs
2 egg yolks
4 tablespoons double cream
fresh strawberries and orange slices, to decorate

To make the base, sift the flour and sugar into a bowl. Add the lemon rind. Make a well in the centre. Add the vanilla essence, egg yolk and butter. Work these into the flour mixture, beating until a dough is formed. Wrap the dough in cling film and refrigerate it for at least 1 hour.

Cut a circle of greaseproof paper to fit the bottom of a 23-cm/9-inch loose-bottomed or springform cake tin. Roll out the dough on the paper, and trim it to fit. Reserve the excess dough in cling film in the refrigerator. Transfer the dough circle on the paper to the base of the tin. Bake the base, without the sides, in a preheated moderately hot oven (200°C, 400°F, Gas 6) for 10 minutes. Let cool.

Grease the sides of the tin lightly, and assemble the sides over the base. Roll out the rest of the dough into a strip as wide as the pan is deep, and use it to line the sides of the tin.

To make the filling, beat the cheeses until they are light and fluffy. Beat in the sugar, flour, orange and lemon rinds, lemon juice and vanilla essence. Stir in the eggs and yolks one at a time, then stir in the cream. Turn the mixture into the pastry case, and bake it in a preheated very hot oven (240°C, 475°F, Gas 9) for 10 minutes. Reduce the heat to very cool (110°C, 225°F, Gas ¼), and bake for 1 hour.

Turn off the heat and leave the cake in the oven with the door ajar for 30 minutes. Transfer it to a wire rack and loosen the sides of the tin. Cool and chill in the tin. Decorate with strawberries and orange slices.

PINEAPPLE CHEESECAKE
Serves 10

Never use fresh pineapple in or on cheesecake. Fresh pineapple contains an enzyme called bromelain which digests protein. It "eats" gelatine and casein, so jellies will not set and cheesecakes will separate and collapse if made with fresh pineapple. The enzyme is destroyed by heat, so canned pineapple is safe.

For the base
225 g/8 oz Marie or other semi-sweet biscuits, crushed
75 g/3 oz butter, melted

For the filling
376-g/13¼-oz can crushed pineapple, drained
439-g/15½-oz can pineapple rings, drained
15 g/½ oz gelatine
450 g/1 lb medium-fat soft cheese, at room temperature
4 eggs, separated
450 ml/15 fl oz soured cream
225 g/8 oz sugar
rind and juice of 1 lemon
4 tablespoons flour
angelica pieces to decorate

To make the base, combine the biscuit crumbs and butter. Press the crumbs onto the bottom and about 1 cm/½ inch up the sides of a lightly greased 23-cm/9-inch springform or loose-bottomed cake tin.

To make the filling, drain the crushed pineapple and pineapple rings, reserving the juice. Beat the cheese until it is fluffy. Beat in the egg yolks, soured cream, sugar, lemon juice, crushed pineapple and flour. Beat well until the mixture is smooth. Whisk the egg whites into stiff peaks. Fold them into the cream cheese mixture. Pour the batter into the tin.

Bake the cake in a preheated moderately hot oven (180°C, 350°F, Gas 4) for 1 hour. Turn off the oven and leave the cake in the oven for another hour. Then leave the oven door ajar 30 minutes more before removing the cake from the oven. Let the cake cool in the tin.

Arrange the pineapple rings and angelica on top of the cheesecake. Combine the reserved pineapple juice with the gelatine over low heat, stirring until the gelatine is completely dissolved (or dissolve the gelatine in the juice in a microwave oven). Let the jelly cool and spoon it over the cake as it is about to set. Refrigerate immediately.

BIBINKA
Serves 8 to 10

This Filipino cheesecake consists of a deliciously light sponge covered with a crust of Edam cheese, an unusual, but delicious, combination. Coconut milk, if unavailable at supermarkets, can be bought in delicatessens and in Indian or West Indian grocers.

400-ml/14-oz can unsweetened coconut milk
175 g/6 oz sugar
3 eggs, beaten
225 g/8 oz plain flour
2 teaspoons baking powder
1 teaspoon bicarbonate of soda
1 teaspoon salt
100 g/4 oz Edam cheese
100 g/4 oz butter
4 tablespoons dessicated coconut
4 tablespoons caster sugar
Glacé cherries to decorate

Line a 23-cm/9-inch springform or loose-bottomed tin with greaseproof paper. Stir the coconut milk (it usually separates in the can) until well blended. Add the sugar and stir well, then stir in the beaten eggs. Sift the flour, baking powder, bicarbonate of soda and salt into a bowl. Beat the flour mixture into the coconut milk mixture until smooth. Pour the combined mixture into the tin and bake in a moderately hot oven (190°C, 375°F, Gas 5) for 45 minutes.

Meanwhile, grate the cheese on a fine grater and melt the butter. Sprinkle the cheese evenly over the cake and return it to the oven. Bake for another 15 minutes, then pour half the butter over it. Bake for a further 15 minutes and pour the rest of the butter over the cake. Bake for another 15 minutes.

Remove the cake from the oven. Combine the dessicated coconut and caster sugar and sprinkle the mixture over the cake. Let the cake cool in the tin. Decorate with glacé cherries.

APPLE SPICE CHEESECAKE
Serves 10 to 12

This is a delicious winter cheesecake, ideal as a dinner party dessert or a coffee break.

For the base
100 g/4 oz ginger biscuits, crushed
100 g/4 oz bran flakes, crushed
50 g/2 oz butter, melted

For the filling
450 g/1 lb low-fat soft cheese
450 ml/¾ pint soured cream
175 g/6 oz soft brown sugar
½ teaspoon ground ginger
½ teaspoon ground cinnamon
½ teaspoon ground cloves
½ teaspoon ground allspice
½ teaspoon ground mace
3 eggs, separated
50 g/2 oz flour

For the topping
1 red skinned apple
1 green skinned apple
1 glacé cherry
2 tablespoons lemon juice
2 tablespoons apricot jam, warmed and sieved

To make the base, combine the ingredients and spread them over the base of a 23-cm/9-inch loose-bottomed tin or springform tin.

To make the filling, beat the cheese with the soured cream, brown sugar, spices and egg yolks. Sift the flour over the mixture and beat it in. Whisk the whites until they are stiff and fold them into the cheese mixture. Pour the mixture into the tin and bake it in a preheated moderate oven (180°C, 350°F, Gas 4) for 1 hour.

Cool it in the oven for another hour, then remove to a rack and cool completely before removing the sides of the tin. When the cake is cool, core and slice the apples evenly. Sprinkle them thoroughly with the lemon juice. Arrange them in a circle round the top of the cake and place the cherry in the centre. Brush with apricot glaze.

PRALINE CHEESECAKE
Serves 10

Pecan nuts are imported from the United States and are not always available; if they are not, substitute walnuts.

For the base
100 g/4 oz chopped mixed nuts
100 g/4 oz digestive biscuits, crushed
3 tablespoons dark brown sugar
3 tablespoons melted butter

For the filling
900 g/2 lb full-fat soft cream cheese, at room
   temperature
175 g/6 oz dark brown sugar
175 g/6 oz white sugar
3 tablespoons dark rum
¼ teaspoon salt
4 large eggs
100 g/4 oz pecan nuts, chopped

For the topping
475 ml/16 fl oz soured cream
50 g/2 oz brown sugar
1 teaspoon dark rum
1 teaspoon maple flavouring

Decoration
150 ml/¼ pint double cream, whipped
pecan nuts

Combine the ingredients for the base and use them to line the base and sides of an ungreased 23-cm/9-inch springform tin.

To make the filling, beat the cream cheese with the sugars until light and fluffy. Add the rum and salt, and beat in the eggs one at a time until well blended. Stir in the nuts. Transfer the mixture to the tin and bake in a preheated moderate oven (180°C, 350°F, Gas 4) for 50 minutes.

Remove it from the oven and let it stand at room temperature while you prepare the topping. Combine the topping ingredients and pour them over the cake. Return the cake to the oven and bake it for 10 minutes. Let the cake cool and then chill it. Remove from the tin and decorate with whipped cream and pecan nuts just before serving.

COFFEE CHEESECAKE
Serves 8 to 10

The most elegant decorations for this cake are coffee-flavoured sweets in the shape of coffee beans. The hint of liqueur and orange in the cake nicely complements the coffee flavour.

For the base
50 g/2 oz butter, softened
50 g/2 oz caster sugar
175 g/6 oz self-raising flour
1 teaspoon baking powder
1 teaspoon grated orange rind
juice of 1 orange

For the filling
75 g/3 oz butter
175 g/6 oz sugar
2 tablespoons instant coffee
1 tablespoon boiling water
1 tablespoon orange juice
2 tablespoons Tia Maria
4 eggs
50 g/2 oz plain flour
75 g/3 oz sultanas
500 g/18 oz full-fat soft cheese, at room temperature
250 ml/8 fl oz double cream

Decoration
150 ml/¼ pint double cream, whipped
chocolate coffee beans

To make the base, beat the butter and sugar until smooth. Sift the flour and baking powder over the mixture and add the orange rind. Stir well. Spread the mixture over the base of a greased 20-cm/8-inch loose-bottomed cake tin. Bake for 10 minutes in a preheated moderate oven (160°C, 325°F, Gas 3).

To make the filling, beat the butter and sugar until they are light and fluffy. Dissolve the coffee in the boiling water; add the orange juice. Allow to cool, then beat into the butter and sugar mixture. Beat in the Tia Maria and the eggs, one at a time. Fold in the flour and sultanas. Put the cheese into a separate bowl and beat it until smooth. Gradually beat in the cream. Fold this mixture into the butter mixture and beat until smooth. Transfer the mixture to the tin.

Bake the cheesecake in a preheated moderate oven (160°C, 325°F, Gas 3) for 1½ hours. Turn the heat off and allow the cake to cool for 1 hour in the oven with the door open. Cool gradually on a wire rack, then chill. Decorate with whipped cream swirled over the top and chocolate coffee beans.

CRUMB CHEESECAKE
Serves 10

This is a very popular, plain cheesecake. Any kind of crumbs can be used for the base and topping, digestive biscuits or crumbled trifle sponge, for instance. To turn this into a special occasion cake, bake it without the topping. While it is still warm, spread it with jam or preserves, then sprinkle with the reserved topping mixture.

For the base and topping
225 g/8 oz bran flakes, crushed
75 g/3 oz demerara sugar
50 g/2 oz butter, melted

For the filling
450 g/1 lb cottage cheese, sieved
50 g/2 oz butter, melted
2 eggs, beaten
2 tablespoons double cream
pinch of salt
100 g/4 oz caster sugar
grated rind and juice of 1 lemon
6 tablespoons flour, sifted

Line a 23-cm/9-inch springform tin with greased greaseproof paper. Combine the crushed cereal and demerara sugar. Reserve one-third of the mixture. Combine the butter with the remaining two-thirds, and use this to line the base of the tin.

To make the filling, combine the cottage cheese with the butter. Beat in the eggs, one at a time. Beat in the rest of the ingredients, in the order given. Pour the mixture into the prepared tin. Cover it with the reserved crumbs. Bake the cake in a preheated moderate oven (180°C, 350°F, Gas 4) for 45 minutes. Cool and chill. Remove from the tin just before serving. Serve chilled.

POPPYSEED CHEESECAKE
Serves 10 to 12

This is the sort of cake that the ancient Greeks ate at weddings and the Romans enjoyed at their feasts. The poppyseeds should be freshly ground, either in the shop or in a coffee grinder at home. Bulghur, also known as pourgouri, is a partially cooked cracked wheat, one of the oldest foods known to man.

For the base
100 g/4 oz bulghur
1 tablespoon clear honey
25 g/1 oz butter

For the filling
4 tablespoons double cream
½ teaspoon ground cinnamon
100 g/4 oz ground black poppyseeds
250 g/8 oz thick honey
1 tablespoon brandy
5 eggs, separated
750 g/1½ lb Mizithra, Ricotta, or low-fat soft cheese
50 g/2 tablespoons flour

For the topping
100 g/4 oz ground black poppyseeds
2 tablespoons brown sugar
50 g/2 oz butter
1 tablespoon brandy
1 tablespoon cornflour

Line the base of a 23-cm/9-inch springform or loose-bottomed tin with greaseproof paper, and grease the sides. Rinse the bulghur in water, squeezing it to remove excess moisture. Put it into a saucepan with the rest of the ingredients. Add 4 tablespoons water and bring to the boil, stirring until all the liquid has been absorbed. Spread the mixture evenly over the base of the tin and allow to cool while you make the filling.

Put the double cream, cinnamon, poppyseeds and honey into a saucepan. Bring to the boil, stirring constantly, until the mixture thickens. Add the brandy and remove from the heat. Allow to cool. When it is cold, beat in the egg yolks, flour and cheese. Whisk the egg whites until stiff, then fold them into the mixture. Turn the mixture into the tin and bake it in a preheated moderate oven (180°C, 350°F, Gas 4) for 45 minutes. Increase the heat to hot oven (220°C, 425°F, Gas 7), and bake for 10 minutes or until the cake is firm in the centre.

Remove the cake from the oven and let it cool at room temperature while you prepare the topping. Combine the topping ingredients and stir them over a low heat until the butter melts and the mixture thickens. Pour it over the cake, then return the cake to the oven and bake for 10 minutes. Remove from oven, cool and chill.

MARBLED CHEESECAKE
Serves 10 to 12

Since this cake is finished off at a very low oven temperature, it needs less time to cool inside the oven when baked. The marble effect looks most impressive but is quite easy to achieve.

For the base
175 g/6 oz digestive biscuits, crushed
3 tablespoons sugar
50 g/2 oz melted butter

For the filling
675 g/1½ lb medium-fat soft cheese, at room temperature
175 g/6 oz caster sugar
3 tablespoons flour
1 teaspoon vanilla essence
3 eggs
50 g/2 oz dark chocolate

To make the base, combine the biscuit crumbs, sugar and butter. Spread the mixture evenly over the base of a greased 23-cm/9-inch springform tin. Bake the base in a preheated (180°C, 350°F, Gas 4) oven for 10 minutes. Remove the pan from the oven and increase the temperature to 230°C, 450°F, Gas 8.

Beat the cheese until fluffy. Beat in the sugar, flour and vanilla essence. Beat in the eggs, one at a time, until well blended. Measure out 250 ml/8 fl oz of the mixture into a small bowl. Melt the chocolate in a bowl over hot water. Stir it into the mixture in the small bowl. Blend well. Carefully spoon alternate layers of the white and brown mixtures over the base. Swirl the combined mixture with a knife to obtain the marbled effect.

Bake the cake in the preheated hot oven (230°C, 450°F, Gas 8) for 10 minutes. Then reduce the heat to very cool (120°C, 250°F, Gas ½) and bake for another 30 minutes. Let the cake cool in the oven for 15 minutes. Loosen the rim of the tin and allow the cake to cool completely, then chill it. Do not remove the rim until the cake is to be served.

RICH CHOCOLATE CHEESECAKE

Serves 10 to 12

This icing can, of course, be used on a wide variety of other cakes.

For the base
175 g/6 oz chocolate bourbon biscuits, crushed
2 tablespoons sugar
3 tablespoons melted butter

For the filling
450 g/1 lb Philadelphia cream cheese, at room temperature
175 g/6 oz sugar
2 tablespoons milk
½ teaspoon vanilla essence
100 g/4 oz dark chocolate
3 eggs

For the icing
225 g/8 oz Philadelphia cream cheese, at room temperature
1 tablespoon milk
1 teaspoon vanilla essence
¼ teaspoon salt
450 g/1 lb icing sugar, sifted
175 g/6 oz dark cooking chocolate
toasted flaked almonds

To make the base, combine the biscuit crumbs, sugar and butter and use the mixture to line a greased 23-cm/9-inch springform tin. Bake the mixture in a preheated moderate oven (160°C, 325°F, Gas 3) for 10 minutes.

To make the filling, beat the cheese and sugar with the milk and vanilla essence. Melt the chocolate in a bowl over hot water and beat it into the mixture. Add the eggs one at a time, beating after each addition. Pour the mixture over the base and bake the cake in a preheated moderate oven (160°C, 325°F, Gas 3) for 40 minutes. Cool the cake in the oven for 1 hour before removing it and loosening the rim. Cool, then chill. Decorate just before serving.

To make the icing, first melt the chocolate. Meanwhile, beat the cream cheese, milk, vanilla and salt until thoroughly blended. Add the sifted icing sugar gradually, beating well after each addition. Stir in the melted chocolate and beat well. Use a palette knife to cover the cake with the icing. Sprinkle toasted flaked almonds around the edge.

PUMPKIN CHEESECAKE
Serves 10 to 12

Pumpkin pie is a favourite American dish. If you want to avoid using canned pumpkin, wrap a large slice of pumpkin (about 750 g/1½ lb) in foil, and bake it in a moderately hot oven (190°C, 375°F, Gas 5) for 1 hour. Scrape away any fibrous material in the centre, and peel the pumpkin. Purée it in a food processor or sieve and weigh out 450 g/1 lb.

For the base
65 g/2½ oz butter, softened
65 g/2½ oz sugar
1 egg
150 g/5 oz flour

For the filling
450 g/1 lb Philadelphia cream cheese, at room temperature
175 g/6 oz caster sugar
450 g/1 lb canned puréed pumpkin, drained
1 teaspoon ground cinnamon
¼ teaspoon ground ginger
¼ teaspoon grated nutmeg
¼ teaspoon salt
2 eggs

Decoration
150 ml/¼ pint double cream, whipped
small marzipan fruits

To make the base, cream the butter and sugar until smooth. Beat in the egg. Sift the flour into the mixture and mix well. Roll out the dough on a sheet of floured greaseproof paper and use it to line the bottom and 5 cm/2 inches up the sides of a 23–cm/9–inch springform tin. Bake the base in a preheated hot oven (200°C, 400°F, Gas 6) for 5 minutes.

To make the filling, combine the cream cheese with the sugar until well blended. Blend in the pumpkin, spices and salt. Add the eggs one at a time, blending well after each addition. Pour the filling into the tin. Bake the cheesecake in a moderate oven (180°C, 350°F, Gas 4) for 50 minutes. Let it cool for 1 hour before removing from the oven. Loosen the rim of the tin. Cool, then chill the cake, but do not remove the rim until just before serving. Decorate with piped whipped cream and marzipan fruits.

LIME CHEESECAKE
Serves 10 to 12

Now that fresh limes are available all year round, more advantage should be taken of them. They are the most delicious of all citrus fruits, because they have such a fragrant taste and smell and are sweeter than lemons.

For the base
225 g/8 oz Marie or other semi–sweet biscuits, crushed
100 g/4 oz butter, melted
100 g/4 oz icing sugar

For the filling
900 g/2 lb cream cheese
350 g/12 oz sugar
rind and juice of 2 limes
pinch of salt
4 large eggs
green food colouring, optional
2 thinly sliced limes, to decorate

To make the base, combine the ingredients and use them to line the base and sides of a 23–cm/9–inch ungreased springform tin.

To make the filling, beat the cheese and sugar together. Beat in the lime juice, rind and salt. Beat in the eggs, one at a time, beating just until the mixture is smooth. Add a few drops of green colouring, if desired. Pour the filling into the prepared crust and bake it in a preheated moderate oven (180°C, 350°F, Gas 4) for 50 minutes. Cool and chill. When the cake is cold, decorate with slices of lime.

WHITE CHOCOLATE CHEESECAKE

Serves 10 to 12

This cake is popular in the United States, where cheesecakes grow every year richer and more elaborate. You can use white chocolate-flavoured cake covering instead of genuine white chocolate, but the flavour will not be as good.

For the base
75 g/3 oz flour
2 tablespoons cocoa powder
50 g/2 oz icing sugar
50 g/2 oz butter, softened
1 egg yolk

For the filling
900 g/2 lb full-fat cream cheese
225 g/8 oz sugar
2 tablespoons white rum
100 g/4 oz white chocolate
pinch of salt
4 large eggs

For the topping
475 ml/16 fl oz soured cream
50 g/2 oz icing sugar
1 teaspoon Triple Sec liqueur
chocolate caraque or
   chocolate flake,
   to decorate

To make the base, sift the flour, cocoa and icing sugar into a bowl. Add the butter and egg yolk, and beat until the mixture is smooth. Roll it out on a piece of greaseproof paper cut to fit a 23-cm/9-inch spring-form pan. Leave enough dough to press it 1 cm/½ inch up the sides of the pan. Refrigerate until required.

To make the filling, whip the cheese with the sugar until light and fluffy. Beat in the rum. Grate the white chocolate and melt it in a basin over simmering water. Beat the melted chocolate into the mixture until smooth. Add salt and beat in the eggs one at a time, whipping only until the eggs are smoothly incorporated. Pour the mixture into the prepared tin and bake in a preheated moderate oven (180°C, 350°F, Gas 4) for 50 minutes.

Remove from the oven and let the cake stand at room temperature while you prepare the topping. Combine the topping ingredients and pour them over the cake. Return the cake to the oven for 10 more minutes. Cool and chill. Decorate with chocolate caraque or chocolate flake. Unmould just before serving.

RICOTTA RING
Serves 8

This cake is baked in a savarin mould or kugelhupf tin. These tins with a hole in the middle are often supplied as part of the "set" when you buy a springform tin. Otherwise, they are to be found in the continental range of bakeware at good cookware stores.

This cake is ideal for baking in a microwave oven. Bake it in a plastic ring mould (such as you might otherwise use for jelly), covered with cling film, for 12 minutes. Of course, in a microwave oven you do not have to bother with the tin of hot water.

grated rind of 1 lemon
175 g/6 oz sugar
450 g/1 lb ricotta cheese
2 large eggs, at room temperature
½ teaspoon vanilla essence
225 g/8 oz fresh or frozen and thawed
  raspberries

Grate the lemon rind and combine it with the sugar. Beat in the cheese, eggs and vanilla essence. Blend thoroughly. Pour the mixture into a well-greased 1.75-litre/3-pint savarin or kugelhupf tin. Cover it with aluminium foil. Place the tin in a baking tin containing enough hot water to come two-thirds of the way up the sides. Bake in a preheated moderate oven (180°C, 350°F, Gas 4) for 1 hour. Cool with the oven door ajar for 30 minutes. Remove from the oven and unmould like a jelly. Refrigerate immediately to prevent cracking and sinking. Just before serving, fill the centre of the ring with the raspberries.

UNBAKED CLASSIC CHEESECAKES

Not all cheesecakes need to be baked. One can achieve a very similar effect by using ingredients, such as gelatine, that need chilling, rather than baking, to make them set. Like baked cheesecakes, unbaked classic cheesecakes are at their best twenty-four hours after being made. Some of them can be frozen, but those which contain gelatine do not freeze well. Always soften gelatine in warm water for about five minutes, then heat it gently to dissolve it, without letting it boil. Gelatine must be completely blended into the other ingredients, or it will form lumpy streaks in the mixture. You can use a microwave oven to melt the butter for the base and to soften the gelatine for the filling. Follow manufacturer's instructions for these operations. Toppings and decorations should be added not more than two hours before serving. Do not serve on hot plates!

CITRUS CHEESECAKE

Serves 8

This is a lovely winter cheesecake, when satsumas and tangerines are in season. If you can find kumquats, which look like miniature oranges, they make a lovely decoration and can be eaten whole, skins included.

For the base
175 g/6 oz chocolate digestive biscuits, crushed
50 g/2 oz melted butter

For the filling
135-g/4¾-oz packet lemon jelly
225 g/8 oz Philadelphia cream cheese, at room temperature
150 ml/¼ pint soured cream
100 g/4 oz caster sugar
½ teaspoon vanilla essence
250 ml/8 fl oz double cream

Decoration
12 tangerine or mandarin segments or 8 kumquats, sliced
1 standard size chocolate flake

Grease a 23-cm/9-inch springform tin. Combine the base ingredients and spread evenly over the base of the tin. Dissolve the jelly in 150 ml/¼ pint hot water. Let it cool. Beat the cheese until fluffy, then beat in the soured cream, sugar and vanilla essence. Whip the cream until it thickens. Fold it into the cheese mixture. Fold the jelly into the mixture. Turn the mixture into the tin and smooth with a palette knife. Chill until set. Decorate with the tangerine or mandarin segments or kumquat slices. Cut the chocolate flake bar into 1-cm/½-inch pieces and use it to decorate the cake.

PEACH CHEESECAKE
Serves 10

This cake has a very peachy flavour, offset by the ginger-flavoured base. When fresh peaches are in season, slice them and use them for the topping, sprinkled with lemon juice to prevent browning.

For the base
75 g/3 oz butter
175 g/6 oz ginger snaps, crushed

For the filling
175 g/6 oz Philadelphia cream cheese
75 g/3 oz caster sugar
2 eggs, separated
3 teaspoons powdered gelatine
410-g/14½-oz can sliced peaches, drained
150 ml/5 fl oz peach-flavoured yogurt
150 ml/5 fl oz double cream
5 drops peach flavouring essence (optional)

Decoration
150 ml/¼ pint double cream, whipped
chocolate sugar strands

Melt the butter and combine it with the ginger snap crumbs. Use the mixture to line the base of a greased 20-cm/8-inch springform or loose-bottomed cake tin. Refrigerate until required.

Beat the cheese with 50 g/2 oz of the sugar until it is fluffy. Beat in the egg yolks. Soften the gelatine in 4 tablespoons of water for 15 minutes. Place the bowl over a saucepan of hot water, and stir until dissolved. Add the gelatine to the cheese mixture and beat well. Chop the peaches into small pieces and fold them into the cheese mixture. Stir in the yogurt and peach flavouring, if used. Whip the cream into soft peaks and fold it into the mixture. Chill the mixture until it is starting to set.

Whisk the egg whites into soft peaks; whip the rest of the sugar into them and fold this meringue into the cheese mixture. Transfer the mixture to the prepared tin and return to the refrigerator. Shortly before serving, unmould the cheesecake (see page 6). Pipe rosettes of cream around the top of this cheesecake and sprinkle with chocolate sugar strands.

LIME AND COCONUT CHEESECAKE

Serves 10

For the base
225 g/8 oz ginger snaps, crumbled
75 g/3 oz butter, melted
50 g/2 oz sugar

For the filling
15 g/½ oz powdered gelatine
100 g/4 oz sugar
4 eggs, separated
125 ml/4 fl oz whipping cream
4 limes
75 g/3 oz dessicated coconut
450 g/1 lb cream cheese, at room temperature
125 g/6 oz icing sugar, sifted

Decoration
2 limes
50 g/2 oz flaked coconut, toasted

Grease a 23–cm/9-inch springform tin. Combine the ginger snaps, melted butter and sugar and spread the mixture over the base and 1 cm/½ inch up the sides of the tin. Press the mixture down with the back of a spoon.

In the top of a double boiler over simmering water, combine the gelatine with 3 tablespoons water. Let it soften for 15 minutes, then stir in the sugar. Remove the pan from the heat and stir until the gelatine has completely dissolved. Beat the egg yolks and add them to the gelatine. Grate the rind from 2 limes and squeeze the juice from four limes. Beat in the juice, the rind and the coconut. Let the mixture cool.

Beat the cream cheese until it is light and fluffy. Beat it into the mixture. Then whip the cream until stiff and add it to the mixture. Whisk the egg whites into soft peaks, then fold in the icing sugar. Fold this meringue into the cheese mixture. Pile the mixture into the tin, smoothing the top with a palette knife. Cover the tin with aluminium foil and refrigerate overnight.

The next day, slice the remaining limes and cut each slice in half. Arrange around the base of the cheesecake. Sprinkle the top with toasted coconut.

ICE CREAM CHEESECAKE
Serves 10

Matzo meal is available from the Jewish section of supermarkets. Because it is made from precooked flour, it is very suitable for pie crusts, as it has a nutty flavour. The pie crust can be baked ahead of time and stored for up to a week.

For the pie crust
100 g/4 oz matzo meal
50 g/2 oz butter, melted
2 tablespoons sugar
½ teaspoon ground cinnamon
¼ teaspoon salt

For the filling
450 g/1 lb Philadelphia cream cheese
475 ml/16 fl oz thick natural yogurt
100 g/4 oz honey
1 teaspoon ground cinnamon

For the topping
340 g/12 oz blackcurrant preserve

To make the pie crust, combine the ingredients and use them to line a 23–cm/9–inch foil pie dish or loose-bottomed flan tin. Bake the crust in a preheated moderately hot (190°C, 375°F, Gas 5) oven, for 20 minutes or until golden.

Use an electric beater to combine the cream cheese, yogurt, honey and cinnamon until smooth. Pour the mixture into the crust and cover it with cling film. Freeze it for 4 to 5 hours or until firm.

When ready to serve, ease the foil pie dish away from the pie or remove the flan tin. Spread the pie with the blackcurrant preserve and let stand 10 minutes before serving.

LEMON CHEESECAKE
Serves 12

The lemon flavour is sharper in an unbaked cake, so you may want to add more sugar. Chocolate decorations make a nice colour contrast.

For the base
225 g/8 oz Marie or other semi-sweet biscuits, crushed
75 g/3 oz butter, melted
25 g/1 oz caster sugar

For the filling
15 g/½ oz gelatine
200 g/7 oz full-fat soft cheese, at room temperature
75 g/3 oz caster sugar
2 eggs, separated
grated rind and juice of 1 lemon
6 tablespoons soured cream

Decoration
150 ml/¼ pint double cream, whipped
lemon slices
chocolate shapes or buttons

To make the base, combine the crushed biscuits, butter and sugar. Use the mixture to line the base and 2.5 cm/1 inch up the sides of a 23-cm/9-inch springform tin.

To make the filling, soften the gelatine in 2 tablespoons warm water. While it is softening, beat the cheese and sugar together until smooth. Beat the egg yolks into the cheese mixture, then beat in the soured cream, the lemon rind and the lemon juice. Dissolve the gelatine over boiling water. While it is cooling slightly, whisk the egg whites into stiff peaks. Stir the gelatine into the mixture, beating until smooth. Then fold the egg whites into the mixture. Transfer the mixture to the tin and chill it until it is firm, at least 2 hours. Unmould and decorate with whipped cream, lemon slices and chocolate shapes just before serving.

FROZEN CRANBERRY CHEESECAKE
Serves 12

The best time to make this cheesecake is immediately after Christmas, when cranberry sauce is reduced in price. If you can get whole cranberries in syrup, they are even better, but they need to be ground coarsely before use.

450 g/1 lb cranberry sauce
2 (about 225-g/8-oz) oranges, peeled and
  chopped
50 g/2 oz sugar
50 g/2 oz chopped walnuts
225 g/8 oz Philadelphia cream cheese, at room
  temperature
250 ml/8 fl oz whipping cream
orange slices, pith and peel removed, to
  decorate

Line a 20-cm/8-inch springform tin with non-stick baking paper, covering the base and sides. Combine the cranberry sauce with the chopped oranges, sugar and walnuts. Whip the cheese until light. Whip the cream and combine it with the cheese, blending until smooth. Fold in the fruit and nuts. Pour the mixture into the prepared tin. Freeze overnight. To serve, slice and decorate with orange slices.

CHERRY CHEESECAKE
Serves 12

Other kinds of pie filling can be used for this cake, or you can use stewed or canned fruit thickened with arrowroot or cornflour.

For the base
75 g/3 oz butter, melted
100 g/4 oz demerara sugar
175 g/6 oz digestive biscuits, crushed
50 g/2 oz ground almonds
½ teaspoon ground cinnamon

For the filling
225 g/8 oz Philadelphia cream cheese, at room temperature
175 g/6 oz icing sugar, sifted
1 tablespoon milk
1 teaspoon almond flavouring
100 g/4 oz chopped mixed nuts
250 ml/8 fl oz double cream
2 (400–g/14.1–oz) cans cherry pie filling

To make the base, combine the ingredients and press them over the base of a lightly greased 23–cm/9–inch springform tin or a 20–cm/8–inch loose-bottomed cake tin.

Combine the cream cheese with 100 g/4 oz of the icing sugar, the milk and half the almond flavouring; mix well until blended. Spread the mixture over the base and flatten with a palette knife. Sprinkle with the nuts. Whip the cream with the rest of the icing sugar until stiff peaks form. Pile the cream over the nuts. Add the rest of the almond flavouring to the pie filling. Cover the cream with the pie filling. Chill the cake in the refrigerator for at least 8 hours or overnight. Do not unmould until just before serving.

SPECIAL OCCASION CHEESECAKES

From the preparation point of view, these cakes can fall into any of the categories of sweet cheese cakes mentioned in this book. The only difference is that they are more elaborate, or contain ingredients that are too expensive for everyday baking. Many people find cheesecakes a welcome change from heavy fruitcakes for special occasions. In fact, the ancient Greeks always had cheesecake wedding cakes, which were similar to the Poppyseed Cheesecake (see page 20).

MARSHMALLOW CHEESECAKE
Serves 10

This would make a lovely children's party cake. Since marshmallows contain gelatine, however, the cake cannot be frozen.

For the base
175 g/6 oz trifle sponge biscuits, crumbled
50 g/2 oz melted butter

For the filling
450 g/1 lb pink-and-white marshmallows
6 tablespoons milk
450 g/1 lb Quark or cottage cheese
grated rind and juice of 1 lemon
1 teaspoon vanilla essence
3 drops cochineal or red colouring
250 ml/8 fl oz whipping cream

For the topping
10 marshmallows
250 g/1 oz plain chocolate, melted

Line the base of a deep, loose-bottomed 23-cm/9-inch cake tin with greaseproof paper. Grease the sides of the tin. Combine the ingredients for the base, and press them onto the base and 1 cm/½ inch up the sides of the cake tin.

In a saucepan over low heat, melt the marshmallows with the milk. Pour the mixture into a bowl and let it cool. Chill it until it is slightly thickened. In another bowl, beat the cheese with the lemon rind, lemon juice, vanilla essence and colouring until smooth. Beat the marshmallow mixture again until smooth, then combine it with the cheese mixture. Whip the cream and fold it into the mixture. Pour this over the base. Chill for at least 4 hours. Unmould it just before you add the topping.

Chop the marshmallows in half, using scissors dipped in hot water, and arrange then around the top of the cheesecake. Drizzle chocolate over the centre.

DESERT ISLAND CHEESECAKE

Serves 8 to 10

This is a refreshing change from the fruit cakes or Swiss rolls which usually form the basis of children's party cakes, and the mixture is not too rich. The cake can be prepared well ahead of time except for the jelly and decorations, which should be added no more than six hours before it is to be served. Use the new, brightly coloured jellies for a festive look.

For the base
8 trifle sponges

For the filling
450 g/1 lb curd cheese
50 g/2 oz butter, melted
½ teaspoon vanilla essence
1 teaspoon lemon juice
1 tablespoon cornflour
4 tablespoons condensed milk
2 eggs, separated
50 g/2 oz caster sugar

For the decoration
135 g/4½ oz packet bright blue jelly
300 ml/½ pint water
3 tablespoons demerara sugar
1 trifle sponge
1 fan shaped ice cream wafer
1 cocktail stirrer palm tree
150 ml/¼ pint double
  cream, whipped

Preheat the oven to hot (230°C, 450°F, Gas 8). Line the base of a 23-cm/9-inch springform or loose-bottomed cake tin with greaseproof paper. Grease the paper and sides of the tin. Slice the trifle sponges horizontally in two and arrange them to cover completely the base of the tin.

Beat the cheese until it is fluffy. Beat in the butter with the vanilla essence and lemon juice. Stir the cornflour into the condensed milk, then beat this into the cheese mixture. Beat in the egg yolks, one at a time. Whisk the egg whites until they form soft peaks, then whisk in the sugar. Fold these into the mixture. Turn the mixture into the tin and level the surface with a palette knife. Put the tin into the hot oven, then reduce the heat to moderate oven (180°C, 350°F, Gas 4); bake the cake for 30 minutes. Cool the cake in the oven with the door ajar for 30 minutes.

Remove the cake and let it cool completely before unmoulding it. Cover it loosely with foil and refrigerate it until you are ready to decorate it.

To decorate the cake, dissolve the jelly in the boiling water and pour it into a large shallow dish or baking tray to make a layer of jelly about 0.5 cm/¼ inch deep. Refrigerate until set. Cut the trifle sponge into a boat shape, make a slit in the top and stick the fan wafer into the slit to make the sail. Pipe a border of cream around the top of the cheesecake. Sprinkle the demerara sugar onto the cake to form an island shape and press the palm tree into the cake until firm.

Roughly chop the jelly and spoon it onto the cake to make the sea. Set the boat on the sea.

RICH COFFEE CHEESECAKE

Serves 8

This Italian dessert is called *Torta di Mascarpone*, although it is more a dessert than a cake. Mascarpone is a full-fat, buttery cream cheese, but when sold in this country, it is interspersed with layers of Gorgonzola. Use Melbury cheese instead.

For the filling
3 eggs, separated
250 g/9 oz sugar
450 g/1 lb Mascarpone, Melbury, or Blue
    Cream Cheese, at room temperature
225-g/8-oz packet amaretto or ratafia biscuits
175 ml/6 fl oz strong black coffee
2 tablespoons rum

For the topping
100 g/4 oz coarsely chopped almonds
2 tablespoons water
2 tablespoons sugar
1 teaspoon almond essence

To make the filling, whisk the egg whites into stiff peaks. Gradually beat in half the sugar until the mixture has a thick, creamy consistency. In another bowl, whisk the yolks with the rest of the sugar until light and frothy. Add the cheese and beat until smooth. Fold in the egg white mixture. Arrange a layer of the biscuits in a glass serving bowl. Mix the coffee and rum and sprinkle the biscuits with the liquid. Cover with a layer of the cheese mixture. Add another layer of biscuits, sprinkling them with the liquid. Then add a cheese layer, and continue until all the ingredients are used up, ending with a layer of cheese. Refrigerate the cake while you make the topping.

To make the topping, put the chopped almonds into a small frying pan with the water, sugar and almond essence. Bring the liquid to the boil and, stirring constantly, boil it for 3 minutes, or until the almonds are brown and the liquid is syrupy. Remove the pan from the heat and stir the contents until they have cooled to lukewarm. Sprinkle the warm topping over the cake and chill before serving.

VALENTINE RHUBARB CHEESECAKE

Serves 6

If you can, bake this in a heart-shaped cake tin, lined with foil or greaseproof paper. It can also be baked in a microwave oven in a heart-shaped jelly mould lined with cling film. Early rhubarb is right in season around St. Valentine's Day.

For the base
3 eggs, at room temperature
175 g/6 oz caster sugar
175 g/6 oz butter, melted
2 tablespoons orange juice
75 g/3 ounces self-raising flour
1 teaspoon baking powder

For the filling
450 g/1 lb rhubarb, trimmed and cut into 2.5-cm/1-inch pieces
275 g/10 oz caster sugar
250 g/9 oz full-fat cream cheese
100 ml/4 fl oz double cream or crème fraîche
1 egg
1 egg yolk
2 tablespoons flour

For the topping
225 g/8 oz strawberries, fresh or frozen
2 tablespoons caster sugar
2 tablespoons lemon juice
1 tablespoon cornflour
150 ml/¼ pint double cream, whipped

Line the cake tin with foil, leaving enough overlapping the edge to enable you to lift the cake out by it. Line the base with buttered greaseproof paper. Lightly grease the sides. Beat the eggs and sugar until pale and fluffy, then fold in the melted butter, orange juice, flour and baking powder. Pour the mixture into the tin. Bake it in a preheated moderately hot oven (190°C, 375°F, Gas 5) for 20 minutes (or bake in a microwave oven on high for 6 minutes, turning it during cooking).

Cook the rhubarb with 50 g/2 oz sugar with 2 tablespoons water in a saucepan until soft, about 20 minutes (or cook in a microwave oven on high, covered with cling film but without extra water, for 4 minutes). Reserve half the rhubarb. Purée the rest and combine it with the cream cheese, cream, egg, egg yolk and flour. Add it to the cake tin. Bake in a preheated moderate oven (180°C, 350°F, Gas 4) for 40 minutes (or bake in a microwave oven for 12 minutes on high). Leave in the oven for 30 minutes with the door ajar. Cool, then chill in the tin.

To make the topping, purée the strawberries with any juice from the reserved rhubarb, the caster sugar and lemon juice. Stir in the cornflour and cook in a double boiler until the sauce thickens. Remove it from the heat, add the reserved rhubarb, and let it cool.

Just before the cake is to be served, unmould it, using the foil to lift it out of the tin. Pipe a border of cream around the top, and fill the centre with the rhubarb and strawberry mixture. Secure a pink or red ribbon around the side of this cheesecake.

GRASSHOPPER FUDGE CHEESECAKE
Serves 12

This extra-rich, liqueur-flavoured cheesecake re-creates a rich American cheescake made in Medford, Oregon, and sent all over the United States at Christmas. In the United States the base is made from Oreo biscuits, which are almost charcoal-coloured, to contrast with the green interior of the cake. Elsewhere a similar effect can be achieved by adding coffee essence.

For the base
175 g/6 oz chocolate bourbon biscuits, crushed
75 g/3 oz plain dessert chocolate
1 teaspoon coffee essence

For the filling
**450 g/1 lb full-fat soft cheese, at room
   temperature**
**450 g/1 lb low-fat soft cheese, at room
   temperature**
175 g/6 oz caster sugar
4 eggs, beaten
250 ml/8 fl oz soured cream
1 tablespoon crème de cacao
1 tablespoon crème de menthe
3 drops green food colouring
6 tablespoons flour

For the topping
225 g/8 oz sugar
150 ml/¼ pint water
**175 g/6 oz plain dessert chocolate, broken into
   pieces**
50 g/2 oz butter

Line the base of a 23-cm/9-inch springform or loose-bottomed tin with greaseproof paper; grease the sides of the tin. Put the ingredients for the base into a saucepan and stir over low heat until the biscuit filling and the chocolate have dissolved (or follow instructions for melting chocolate in a microwave oven). Spread the mixture over the base and chill.

Use an electric mixer to mix the filling ingredients, adding them in the order given, and beating well after each addition. Pour the filling into the tin. Bake the cake in a preheated moderate oven (180°C, 350°F, Gas 4) for 1 hour. Let it cool in the oven with the door ajar for 1 hour. Cool on a wire rack, unmould, then chill thoroughly before covering with the topping.

To make the topping, put the sugar and water into a saucepan and stir over gentle heat until the sugar has dissolved. Bring it to the boil and boil gently, without stirring, for 5 minutes. Remove the pan from the heat and stir in the chocolate pieces and butter. Beat with a wooden spoon, until the chocolate and butter have dissolved and the mixture is thick and glossy. Swirl it over the cake with a palette knife.

PASKHA (RUSSIAN EASTER CAKE)

Serves 10

This traditional cheesecake used to be made in a wooden mould known as a Turk's head, because it bore a vague resemblance to a fez. The words *khristos voskresye,* "Christ has risen" in Russian, were written on the side in candied fruit. You will need layers of cheesecloth (see page 4) and a tall clay flowerpot. Rosewater is available at chemists and at Middle Eastern grocers.

750 g/1½ lb full-fat curd cheese
100 g/4 oz unsalted butter, softened
2 egg yolks
100 g/4 oz sugar
½ teaspoon rosewater
175 ml/6 fl oz soured cream
50 g/2 oz blanched chopped almonds
100 g/4 oz seedless raisins
100 g/4 oz chopped mixed candied fruit
50 g/2 oz glacé cherries, chopped
50 g/2 oz chopped mixed candied peel

Decoration
glacé fruits
1 glacé cherry
50 g/2 oz chopped mixed candied fruit

Line a clean, new flowerpot with a large piece of cheesecloth. The cloth should be large enough to cover the insides of the pot and then cover the cheese when potted. Press the cloth firmly against the sides of the pot, and let the excess hang over the edge.

Beat the cheese in a bowl until it is fluffy. Beat in the butter. In a separate bowl beat the eggs and sugar until light and pale-coloured, then beat in the rosewater. Beat the egg mixture into the cheese mixture, then beat in the soured cream. Toast the almonds in a dry frying pan over high heat, stirring until the almonds give off their aroma. Stir the toasted almonds into the cheese mixture. Stir in the candied fruit, cherries and peel, making sure all are evenly distributed. Turn the mixture into the lined flowerpot. Fold the edges of the cheesecloth over the filling. Place a saucer on top and weigh it down with a 1-kg/2-lb weight or can. Stand the pot in the refrigerator on a strong oven rack (such as the rack from the grill pan), with a saucer underneath it to catch the whey as it drips out. Chill for 24 hours.

To unmould the cheesecake, remove the weight and saucer. Uncover the cheese mixture. Invert a flat plate over it and then turn the pot upside down onto the plate. Carefully remove the cheesecloth, then decorate with the glacé fruits, chopped candied fruit and glacé cherry.

CREAM CHEESE YULE LOG
Serves 8

For the Swiss roll
3 eggs
100 g/4 oz sugar
100 g/4 oz flour
2 teaspoons boiling water

For the filling and topping
225 g/8 oz full-fat soft cheese
225 g/8 oz curd cheese
225 g/8 oz cottage cheese
2 tablespoons natural yogurt
225 g/8 oz caster sugar
1 teaspoon Kirsch (optional)
100 g/4 oz candied fruit, chopped
2 teaspoons Cointreau or tropical fruit juice
Christmas ornaments and holly, to decorate

To make the Swiss roll, line the base of a Swiss roll tin with greaseproof paper. Grease the sides of the tin. Whisk the eggs and sugar until light and fluffy. Sift in the flour and stir lightly. Add the boiling water and stir again. Pour the mixture into the tin and bake in a preheated moderately hot oven (200°C, 400°F, Gas 6) for 7 minutes.

Slide the Swiss roll out of the tin on its backing paper. Whip the cheeses together with the yogurt until light and fluffy. Beat in the sugar and Kirsch, if used. Divide the mixture into two portions, one twice as big as the other. Stir the candied fruits into the smaller portion. Sprinkle the cooled Swiss roll with the Cointreau or fruit juice. Use a palette knife to spread the cheese-and-candied-fruit mixture in an even layer over the roll. Roll up the Swiss roll, pulling the backing paper away as you do so. Lay it on the dish on which it will be served. Use the palette knife to spread the outside of the roll with the rest of the cheese. When it is smooth, run the tines of a fork along the "log" to represent the wood grain.

RICH ROMAN CHEESECAKE
Serves 10

The forerunner of this cheesecake was invented by the ancient Romans. This "modern" version is several hundred years old, but contains ingredients unknown to the Romans, such as sugar.

For the pastry dough
225 g/8 oz flour, sifted
175 g/6 oz salted butter
4 egg yolks
50 g/2 oz caster sugar
1 tablespoon Marsala *or* sherry
1 teaspoon grated lemon rind
pinch of salt

For the filling
900 g/2 lb ricotta *or* sieved cottage cheese
4 tablespoons double cream
100 g/4 oz caster sugar
1 tablespoon flour
½ teaspoon salt
1 teaspoon vanilla essence
1 teaspoon grated orange rind
4 egg yolks
1 tablespoon sultanas
2 tablespoons candied peel, chopped
2 tablespoons blanched almonds, slivered
1 egg white beaten with 1 tablespoon water

To make the pastry dough, sift the flour and beat in the butter, egg yolks, sugar, Marsala or sherry, lemon rind and salt. Beat the dough, then knead it into a ball. Wrap it in cling film and refrigerate it for at least 30 minutes.

Cut out a piece of greaseproof paper to fit a 23-cm/9-inch springform tin. Sprinkle the paper with flour. Divide the dough into four equal parts. Return one part to the refrigerator and knead the other three parts together briefly. Roll out the dough to a thickness of 5 mm/¼ inch over the paper to fit the base of the tin. Trim off any excess dough and reserve it. Place the dough on the paper in the tin. Roll out the rest of the dough into a 10-cm/4-inch wide strip, and use it to line the inside of the rim, draping it over a rolling pin to insert into the tin. Press the base and sides of the dough together, sealing them so they will hold in the filling.

Put the cheese, cream, sugar, flour, salt, vanilla essence, orange rind and yolks into a bowl and beat well until smooth. Stir in the sultanas, candied peel and almonds. Transfer the mixture to the pastry-lined tin and smooth the surface with a palette knife.

Roll out the reserved dough into a rectangle about 25 cm/10 inches by 15 cm/6 inches. Cut it into 1-cm/½-inch strips. Brush it with the lightly beaten egg white. Arrange the strips in a lattice pattern over the cake. Bake it in a preheated moderate oven (180°C, 350°F, Gas 4) for 1¼ hours, or until the crust is golden. Cool the cake in the oven for 1 hour, then cool on a wire rack. The rim can be removed before chilling. Chill for at least 24 hours before serving.

SAVOURY CHEESECAKES

Some of these look just like the classic cheesecakes and are prepared in the same way except that the flavouring is savoury and not sweet. These are ideal for an elegant and unusual starter or for a cold buffet. There are also cheese breads, pies, pastries, and tarts. The new flavoured soft cheeses, such as herb cheeses and garlic cheeses, work well in cheesecakes. Use one of these classic cheesecakes as a basis for the proportion of ingredients and substitute a flavoured soft cheese for plain soft cheese as, for instance, in the recipe for Smoked Salmon Cheesecake.

CAVIAR PIE
Serves 8

The smooth white surface of the pie is ideal for garnishing with raw vegetables: tomato, spring onion, parsley, or anything edible. Don't worry, you don't *have* to use real caviar!

2 bunches (about 175 g/6 oz) spring onions
6 hard–boiled eggs
2 tablespoons melted butter
salt and pepper
100 g/4 oz lumpfish *or* other black fish roe
225 g/8 oz Philadelphia *or* Quark cheese, at
   room temperature
100 g/4 oz natural yogurt

garnish
2 radish roses
1 spring onion palm tree

Top and tail the spring onions. Blend them in a food processor with the hard-boiled eggs. Sprinkle with the melted butter, salt and pepper. Press the mixture firmly onto the base and up the sides of a glass or china pie plate or flan dish. Chill for 10 minutes to set.

   Reserve 2 teaspoons lumpfish roe for decoration and spread the remainder over the base. Beat the cheese and yogurt together until fluffy and use a palette knife to spread this carefully over the roe, taking care to keep the layers separate. Garnish with radish roses, spring onion palm tree and reserved lumpfish roe.

SMOKED SALMON CHEESECAKE
Serves 10 to 12

This is another elegant cake which looks more expensive and luxurious than it is. Smoked salmon trimmings are fairly inexpensive and are cheapest when bought at a fishmonger's market stall.

For the base
100 g/4 oz butter
175 g/6 oz high-bake water biscuits, crushed
3 tablespoons chopped parsley
salt and pepper

For the filling
25 g/1 oz powdered gelatine
150 ml/¼ pint water
450 g/1 lb low-fat soft cheese
50 g/2 oz herb-and-garlic-flavoured, full-fat, soft cheese
4 eggs, separated
300 ml/½ pint soured cream
100 g/4 oz smoked salmon trimmings
salt and pepper

Garnish
sliced cucumber
parsley sprig
25 g/1 oz smoked salmon cut into strips

Line the bottom of a 23 cm/9 inch springform tin with greaseproof paper. Grease the sides. Melt the butter in a saucepan and stir in the crushed water biscuits. Remove from the heat, add the parsley and sprinkle with salt and pepper. Press the mixture over the base of the tin.

To make the filling, dissolve the gelatine in the water over gentle heat. Beat the cheeses together until fluffy, then beat in the egg yolks and soured cream. Beat the gelatine into the cheese mixture. Cool, then chill for 30 minutes or until the mixture is on the point of setting. Meanwhile, chop the smoked salmon trimmings, and whisk the egg whites into stiff peaks. Stir the chopped salmon into the mixture and fold in the egg whites. Spoon the mixture into the tin and smooth the top with a palette knife. Refrigerate for at least 4 hours or until required.

Garnish with the sliced cucumber, parsley sprig and smoked salmon strips.

WALNUT CHEESE TEA BREAD
Serves 8

This quick loaf made with baking powder is a nice change for tea time. It can also be baked in the microwave oven, for 8 minutes on full power, in which case add 1 teaspoon gravy browning to the mixture to improve the colour.

225 g/8 oz self-raising flour
1 teaspoon salt
1 teaspoon baking powder
175 g/6 oz butter
75 g/3 oz grated Parmesan cheese
50 g/2 oz walnuts, chopped *or* ground
2 eggs, beaten
150 ml/¼ pint milk

Grease a 900-ml/2-lb loaf tin. Sift the flour, salt and baking powder into a bowl. Cut the butter into pieces and rub it into the flour until the mixture resembles fine bread crumbs. Stir in the cheese, walnuts, eggs and milk. Beat until smooth. Turn the mixture into the loaf tin and smooth the top with a palette knife. Bake in a preheated moderately hot oven (190°C, 375°F, Gas 5) for 1 hour or until a knife inserted into the centre comes out clean. Cool in the tin, then turn out onto a wire rack.

BOUREKAS
Makes about 35 5-cm/2-inch bourekas

These savoury pastries are popular throughout the Middle East. In Turkey, they are known as boreg, and are usually eaten with hard-boiled eggs. Phyllo dough is available from Greek grocers and good supermarkets. It freezes well but will dry out quickly while at room temperature, so always keep whatever dough you are not using at the moment covered with a damp cloth.

225 g/8 oz phyllo dough
100 g/4 oz butter, melted
50 g/2 oz sesame seeds

Cheese filling
450 g/1 lb Feta cheese
2 eggs, beaten
4 tablespoons chopped parsley
½ teaspoon pepper
25 g/1 oz butter, melted

VATRUSHKY
Makes about 30

First, prepare the filling. Crumble the feta with a fork. Add the rest of the ingredients and work them into a paste. Cover and reserve them.

Lay a sheet of phyllo dough on a greased baking tray. Brush it with melted butter. Use a sharp knife to slice the sheet lengthwise into four equal strips. Place 1 teaspoon of the filling about 1 inch from the top left-hand corner of each strip. Fold the corner of dough over the filling, making a triangle, then fold the triangle down over the strip of greased dough and continue folding until the whole forms a triangular package. Lightly brush tops with melted butter, sprinkle with a few sesame seeds and set aside on a greased baking sheet. Repeat the procedure until all the dough and filling have been used up. Bake the pastries in a moderately hot oven (200°C, 400°F, Gas 6) for 20 minutes, or until golden brown. Serve as quickly as possible.

You can make smaller bourekas by cutting each sheet of dough into six, instead of four, strips. The smaller the bourekas, the less baking time they will need. Serve larger bourekas with hard-boiled eggs, smaller ones as cocktail snacks.

Although these Russian tartlets are slightly sweet, they are served with borsch (beetroot soup) and other soups. The cheese is usually homemade (see page 5).

225 g/8 oz chilled butter
450 g/1 lb flour
salt
2 eggs
450 g/1 lb full-fat soft cheese
1 teaspoon sugar

Cut the butter into small pieces and rub it into the flour until the mixture resembles bread crumbs. Add a pinch of salt, one of the eggs and enough cold water to make a fairly firm dough. Wrap it in cling film and leave it in the refrigerator for at least 30 minutes.

Beat the cheese with the other egg, ½ teaspoon salt and the sugar. Roll out the dough until it is about 5 mm/¼ inch thick. Use a fluted pastry cutter to cut it into rounds. Use the rounds to line buttered tartlet tins. Fill each tartlet with 2 teaspoons of the cheese mixture. Bake the tartlets in a preheated hot oven (230°C, 450°F, Gas 8) for 15 minutes or until the pastry is lightly browned.

TYROPITTA
Serves 12

This traditional Greek cheese pie is made with feta cheese and phyllo dough. It can be made in a roasting tin or in a Swiss roll tin with foil placed around the sides, to come 5 cm/2 inches above the top.

350 g/12 oz Feta cheese
225 g/8 oz cream cheese
225 g/8 oz cottage cheese
8 eggs
¼ teaspoon black pepper
1 teaspoon dried dill *or* 1 tablespoon chopped
   fresh dill
2 tablespoons chopped parsley
150 g/5 oz butter, melted
3 tablespoons flour
275 ml/9 fl oz milk
18 sheets phyllo dough

Crumble the feta cheese into a bowl. Add the other cheeses and beat well. Beat in the eggs, pepper and herbs. Melt 3 tablespoons of the butter in a saucepan over gentle heat. Add the flour and cook, stirring for 2 minutes. Add the milk all at once, and stir until the sauce thickens. Remove the sauce from the pan and allow to cool until lukewarm. Then beat it into the cheese mixture.

Line a greased 30 × 25-cm/12 × 10-inch roasting tin with a sheet of phyllo dough. Melt the rest of the butter and brush some over the dough. Cover it with another sheet and brush this sheet with butter. Repeat until you have used 9 sheets of dough, keeping the dough not in use covered with a damp cloth, or it will dry out and become too brittle to use. Pour the cheese mixture over the dough. Cover it with the rest of the phyllo dough, brushing each sheet with the melted butter. Tuck in the edges of the dough around the tin. Use a sharp knife to cut the dough into diamond-shaped serving pieces. Brush the top with the rest of the butter.

Bake the pie in a preheated moderate oven (180°C, 350°F, Gas 4) for 45 minutes, or until the pastry is golden. Serve warm.

BROCCOLI CHEESECAKE

Serves 8

Delicious for a picnic or cold buffet, this cheesecake is the perfect accompaniment to cold meat and salad. Fresh herbs can be added according to season; if fresh are not available, use 2 teaspoons dried mixed herbs.

For the base
175 g/6 oz rye crispbread, crushed
3 tablespoons melted butter
3 tablespoons grated Parmesan cheese
salt and pepper

For the filling
450 g/1 lb cottage cheese, sieved
50 g/2 oz butter, melted
2 eggs
2 tablespoons soured cream
½ teaspoon salt
grated rind and juice of 1 lemon

6 tablespoons flour, sifted
225 g/8 oz broccoli, cooked
¼ teaspoon grated nutmeg

Garnish
2 tomatoes, sliced
grated Parmesan cheese

To make the base, mix the crispbread with the butter and Parmesan cheese, and sprinkle with salt and pepper. Spread the base of a 23-cm/9-inch greased springform tin with the mixture. Chill until required.

Combine the cottage cheese and butter. Beat in the eggs, one at a time, and the soured cream. Add the salt, lemon rind, lemon juice, flour and nutmeg. Beat well. Chop the cooked broccoli and stir it into the mixture, then pour the mixture into the prepared tin.

Bake the cheesecake in a preheated moderate oven (180°C, 350°F, Gas 4) for 45 minutes. Cool in the oven for 1 hour. Chill and serve cold, garnished with tomato slices and grated Parmesan cheese.

CHEESE SCONES
Makes 12

These savoury cheesecakes are as traditional in Britain as Maids of Honour. These scones are richer than sweet scones, so they will probably serve more people. Serve them warm, if possible.

225 g/8 oz self-raising flour
½ teaspoon salt
1 teaspoon bicarbonate of soda
1 teaspoon cream of tartar
50 g/2 oz butter, chilled
50 g/2 oz Cheshire cheese, grated
5 tablespoons soured cream
1 egg beaten

Sift the flour, salt, soda and cream of tartar into a bowl. Rub in the butter until the mixture resembles bread crumbs. Add the grated cheese. Make a well in the mixture and pour in the soured cream and half the beaten egg. Stir and mix to a smooth, spongy dough.

Turn the dough out onto a floured work surface and knead it briefly. Roll it out lightly until it is about 1-cm/½-inch thick. Use a fluted cutter to cut it into rounds. Knead the scraps and cut them into rounds, until all the dough is used up. Place the rounds on greased baking trays. Let them rest 20 minutes.

Mix the rest of the egg with 2 teaspoons of water and brush the mixture over the scones. Bake the scones in a preheated hot oven (230°C, 450°F, Gas 8) for 10 minutes, or until well-risen and golden brown.

CHEESE MERINGUES
Makes 12

These dainty morsels make ideal snacks to be served with drinks, and your guests will have a hard time guessing exactly how they are made!

2 egg whites
½ teaspoon salt
½ teaspoon cream of tartar
1 tablespoon self-raising flour, sifted
50 g/2 oz Parmesan cheese, grated
oil for deep frying
½ teaspoon cayenne
parsley sprigs, to garnish

Whisk the egg whites with the salt and cream of tartar until stiff. Fold in the flour and cheese. Heat the oil to 190°C/375°F or until a 2.5-cm/1-inch cube of bread will brown in 60 seconds. Mould the mixture into ovals between two teaspoons and drop the ovals into the fat. Fry briefly, in batches, removing the meringues as soon as they turn pale brown. Drain on crumpled absorbent kitchen paper. Arrange the meringues on a serving dish and sprinkle them lightly with cayenne. Garnish with parsley sprigs. Serve as soon as possible.

EGG AND CHEESE PIE
Serves 8

This unusual egg and cheese mixture is based on a Moroccan recipe. The original recipe called for 1 tablespoon of cinnamon, but this might be too much for European palates, so I have reduced it. It would be more authentic to use phyllo dough for the pastry, but pizza dough is quicker.

450 g/1 lb pizza dough
225 g/8 oz Feta cheese, crumbled
6 hard–boiled eggs, coarsely chopped
4 tablespoons chopped parsley
4 tablespoons grated onion
1 teaspoon ground cinnamon
1 egg, beaten with 2 teaspoons water

Defrost the dough if it is frozen. Divide it into two pieces. Roll each into a 23–cm/9-inch diameter circle. Lay one circle into a greased 20–cm/8-inch pie dish. Combine the filling ingredients and spread the mixture over the dough. Brush the edge with beaten egg. Cover with the other circle of dough and press well with a fork to make a well-sealed, but decorative, edge. Brush with the egg mixture. Bake the pie in a preheated hot oven (200°C, 400°F, Gas 7) for 30 minutes or until golden brown.

CHEESECAKES WITH A DIFFERENCE

These recipes include pies, small pastries, cakes and strudels, not shaped or baked in the classic cheesecake way. They originate from many countries, including Britain, and illustrate the versatility of cheese as an ingredient in home baking. Cheese is also an ideal replacement for custard as a flan and tart filling, and the slightly sour taste is also excellent for bringing out the flavour of fruit. Do not cook any of these recipes in the microwave oven unless microwaving instructions are specifically included.

QUICK CREAM CHEESE FLAN
Serves 4

Any kind of flan case can be used, including the standard sponge, specified here. If the case is prebaked, the rest of the flan can be cooked for 6 minutes in a microwave oven.

2 eggs
1 egg yolk
500 g/18 oz full-fat soft cheese
grated rind of 1 lemon
50 g/2 oz self-raising flour
50 g/2 oz seedless raisins
1 23-cm/9-inch prebaked flan case
icing sugar for dredging

Beat the eggs, egg yolk, cheese and lemon rind until smooth. Beat in the flour and stir in the raisins. Spoon the mixture into the prepared flan case. Bake in a preheated moderate oven (180°C, 350°F, Gas 4) for 15 minutes or until set and light golden brown. Serve warm dredged with icing sugar.

ALMOND CHEDDAR FLAN
Serves 8

This is a delicious and unusual combination and is not too sweet. Hazelnuts would taste just as good as almonds.

For the base
50 g/2 oz butter
1 tablespoon golden syrup
175 g/6 oz digestive biscuits, crushed

For the filling
100 g/4 oz blanched, coarsely chopped almonds
175 ml/6 fl oz whipping cream
175 g/6 oz Cheddar cheese, finely grated
1 teaspoon lemon juice
50 g/2 oz caster sugar

Grease an 18-cm/7-inch flan ring. Melt the butter and syrup in a saucepan and stir in the crushed biscuits. Mix well, then press into the flan ring evenly to form a base. Refrigerate for 20 minutes while you toast the almonds.

Put the almonds into a dry frying pan. Heat them, stirring occasionally, until they begin to give off their characteristic aroma, then remove them from the heat. They should be lightly browned. Sprinkle half the almonds over the flan base. Whip the cream into soft peaks, then stir in the grated cheese, lemon juice and sugar and whip again lightly. Spread this mixture over the flan base. Refrigerate until required. Before serving, sprinkle with the rest of the almonds.

CREAM CHEESE PASTRY
Makes two 23-cm/9-inch pie shells or 32 5-cm/2-inch tartlets

This is also known as Vienna pastry. It is especially delicious for fruit tarts. This pastry freezes well.

225 g/8 oz flour
½ teaspoon salt
225 g/8 oz Philadelphia cream cheese, chilled
225 g/8 oz butter, chilled

Sift the flour and salt into a bowl. Cut the cream cheese and butter into small pieces and rub them into the flour until the mixture resembles coarse bread crumbs. Add a tablespoon of water and form the dough into a ball. Wrap it in cling film and refrigerate for at least 30 minutes. Divide the dough into two equal parts. Roll out each into a 28-cm/11-inch circle and use it to line two 23-cm/9-inch pie or flan tins. Alternatively, do not divide the dough into two, but roll it out and use it to line two greased 12-cup tart tins. Bake the pastry blind in a preheated hot oven (230°C, 450°F, Gas 8). If you are baking a pie shell, allow 12 to 15 minutes; if you are baking tartlets, allow 8 to 10 minutes. Cool and fill with fresh fruit. Brush with warmed sieved jam.

CHEESE STRUDEL
Makes two 20-cm/8-inch strudels (Serves 16)

Most people are familiar with apple strudel. This alternative filling for strudel is just as popular. Strudel or phyllo dough can be bought ready-made in sheets from Greek and continental bakers and grocers. Strudel dough is actually slightly different from phyllo dough. Both dry out very quickly, so always keep them covered with a damp tea towel when not actually working with them. They freeze very well, but must be defrosted slowly in the refrigerator.

150 g/5 oz butter
100 g/4 oz sugar
4 tablespoons soured cream
225 g/8 oz cottage cheese
225 g/8 oz full-fat soft cheese
1 teaspoon grated lemon rind
3 tablespoons ground almonds
pinch of salt
3 tablespoons sultanas
4 sheets strudel *or* phyllo dough
4 tablespoons dry bread crumbs
icing sugar for dredging

To make the filling, beat half the butter with all but 2 tablespoons of the sugar until creamy. Add the soured cream. Sieve the cottage and cream cheeses, or blend them in a food processor, and add to the mixture. Beat in the almonds, lemon rind and salt. Stir in the sultanas.

Dampen a tea towel. Lay a sheet of dough on the towel. Melt the rest of the butter and brush some evenly over the dough with a pastry brush. Sprinkle the dough with 1 tablespoon of the bread crumbs.

Lay a second sheet of dough on top of the first. Brush this sheet evenly with more melted butter. Combine the rest of the sugar with 2 tablespoons of the bread crumbs. Sprinkle half this mixture over two-thirds of the dough, leaving the third farthest away from you uncovered. Spread half the filling mixture over the same two-thirds of the dough that has been sprinkled with sugar and bread crumbs. Roll up the dough like a Swiss roll, starting at the end nearest to you and finishing with the unfilled third of the dough. Use the tea towel to help transfer the strudel to a greased baking sheet.

Repeat the procedures with the other two sheets of dough, brushing with butter, sprinkling with bread crumbs and sugar, and using up the rest of the filling. Transfer this strudel to the baking sheet. Bake the strudels in a preheated moderately hot oven (190°C, 375°F, Gas 5) for 30 minutes or until the strudels are golden brown. Serve warm or cold, dredged with icing sugar.

CHEESE TURNOVERS ALLA GRANATA

Makes 12

This is a Sicilian recipe adapted by Angelo Granata, whose Salumeria Granata supplies most of London with typical southern Italian pastries baked on the premises. You can, of course, use your own favourite puff pastry recipe instead of using a packet. The better the quality of chocolate used, the better the end result.

360-g/13-oz packet puff pastry
225 g/8 oz Ricotta *or* low-fat curd cheese
4 tablespoons caster sugar
1 tablespoon grated lemon rind
1 egg
100 g/4 oz plain chocolate
25 g/1 oz butter

Roll out the pastry and cut it into 10-cm/4-inch circles. Combine the cheese with the sugar, lemon rind and egg, beating until smooth. Place 1 teaspoon of filling in the centre of each of the circles of dough. Brush the edges with water. Fold each in half, like a turnover. Press lightly to close. Transfer the turnovers to a greased baking sheet; bake them in a preheated, moderately hot oven (200°C, 400°F, Gas 6) for 15 minutes or until browned. Cool the turnovers on wire racks.

While the turnovers are cooling, melt the chocolate and butter in a double boiler over hot water, or in a small bowl in a microwave oven on the lowest setting. Dip half of each turnover into the chocolate mixture. Arrange the turnovers on the edge of racks or plates to cool, so that the chocolate is not touching any surface. Eat cold or chilled.

MAIDS OF HONOUR
Makes 24

These cakes were used by Anne Boleyn to tempt Henry VIII. At least, this is the claim of Dr. Andrew Boorde (1490?–1549). He ought to have been in the know because he was physician to the Duke of Norfolk, Anne Boleyn's uncle and the man who engineered the match. Boorde's recipe reads "take new cheese and grynde hit fayne, in mortar with eggs. Put powdre thereto of sugar, coloure hit with saffron. Put hit in cofyns that be fayre and bake it forthe." This is what he meant:

For the tartlet pastry
225 g/8 oz flour
¼ teaspoon salt
100 g/4 oz butter
2 tablespoons caster sugar
3 tablespoons milk

For the filling
⅛ teaspoon saffron strands
50 g/2 butter
225 g/8 oz sugar
2 eggs
½ teaspoon baking powder
450 g/1 lb curd cheese
¼ teaspoon grated nutmeg
50 g/2 oz currants

Grease two 12-cup tartlet tins. Make the pastry by sifting the flour and salt into a bowl. Cut and rub in the butter until the mixture resembles fine bread crumbs. Stir in the caster sugar and milk, to make a firm dough. Gather it into a ball, wrap it in a plastic bag and refrigerate it for 20 minutes. Roll out the dough and cut it with a pastry cutter to fit the tartlet tins. Line the tins with the dough.

To make the filling dissolve the saffron in 2 teaspoons boiling water. Over low heat, melt the butter and sugar. Beat in the eggs, dissolved saffron, baking powder, curd cheese, nutmeg and currants. Pour the mixture into the prepared pastry cases. Bake the Maids of Honour in a preheated moderate oven (180°C, 350°F, Gas 4) for 30 minutes, or until the pastry is golden.

RUM CHEESE PYES
Makes 24

Here is another traditional English recipe from the Yorkshire dales.

1 quantity Tartlet Pastry (see page 54)
100 g/4 oz butter, softened
225 g/8 oz curd cheese
225 g/8 oz sugar
2 eggs
¼ teaspoon bicarbonate of soda
½ teaspoon vanilla essence
generous pinch of grated nutmeg
1 tablespoon rum

Roll out the Tartlet Pastry (see page 54) to fit two 12-cup greased tartlet tins. Beat the butter, cheese, sugar, eggs, soda and vanilla essence until smooth. Pour the mixture into the pastry, filling the tartlets not more than three-quarters full. Sprinkle with nutmeg and bake in a preheated moderate oven (180°C, 350°F, Gas 4) for 30 minutes, or until the pastry is golden. When cooked, sprinkle with rum.

IRISH CURD CAKE
Serves 8

For the base
1 quantity Tartlet Pastry (see page 54)
1 egg, beaten

For the filling
450 g/1 lb curd cheese, at room temperature
2 eggs, beaten
225 g/8 oz soft brown sugar
grated rind and juice of 1 small lemon
50 g/2 oz seedless raisins

Roll out the pastry (see page 54) and use it to line the base and sides of a greased 20-cm/8-inch flan tin. Prick the pastry all over the base, and bake 10 minutes in a preheated moderately hot oven (190°C, 375°F, Gas 5) or until lightly browned. Remove from the oven and brush the pastry with the beaten egg to prevent the filling from soaking in.

To make the filling, combine the cheese and eggs with 4 tablespoons of the brown sugar, the lemon rind, and lemon juice. Beat until well blended. Stir in the raisins. Turn into the prepared pastry shell. Sprinkle thickly with the rest of the brown sugar. Bake in a preheated moderate oven (180°C, 350°F, Gas 4) for 40 minutes or until the top is well browned. Cool to room temperature before serving.

BISHOP AUCKLAND CHEESECAKES

Makes 24

These cheesecakes are more solid than those from further south, and have a delicious lemony flavour.

1 quantity Tartlet Pastry (see page 54)
100 g/4 oz mashed potato
100 g/4 oz curd cheese
50 g/2 oz melted butter
100 g/4 oz caster sugar
grated rind and juice of 1 lemon
1 egg
100 g/4 oz currants

Grease two 12-cup tartlet tins. Roll out the tartlet pastry (see page 54) and use it to line the tartlet tins. Combine the rest of the ingredients in the order given. Divide the mixture between the pastry cases. Bake them in a preheated moderate oven (190°C, 375°F, Gas 5) for 20 minutes, or until the pastry is golden.

SWALEDALE CHEESECAKE

Serves 8

This is actually a curd cheese flan. Like all cheesecakes, it was seasonal at Whitsuntide.

1 quantity Tartlet Pastry (see page 54)
2 eggs
2 tablespoons double cream
grated rind of 1 lemon
generous pinch of ground nutmeg
100 g/4 oz butter, melted
450 g/1 lb curd cheese
225 g/8 oz sugar
50 g/2 oz currants
2 tablespoons milk
1 teaspoon caster sugar

Grease a 20-cm/8-inch flan or tart tin. Roll out the dough as thinly as possible to fit the tin, reserving some of the dough for the lattice top. Beat the eggs with the cream, lemon rind, nutmeg, melted butter, cheese and sugar, until smooth. Stir in the currants. Pile the mixture into the flan tin. Roll out the reserved dough and cut it into 1-cm/½-inch wide strips. Arrange the strips in a lattice pattern over the filling. Dissolve the sugar in the milk over gentle heat. Brush the lattice with the mixture to glaze it. Bake the tart in a preheated moderate oven (180°C, 350°F, Gas 4) for 30 minutes, or until the pastry is golden.

ALBANIAN CHEESECAKE
(Revani me kos)
Serves 8 to 10

From the typically English, we pass to the typically Albanian! This is a Middle Eastern type of cheesecake, usually made in a very large round tray. This version is more modest in size. The sweetness is counteracted if eaten with a cup of strong Turkish coffee. Orange flower water or rosewater can be bought at any good chemist.

For the cake
225 g/8 oz cottage cheese
250 ml/8 fl oz buttermilk
4 eggs
4 tablespoons melted butter
350 g/12 oz sugar
2 teaspoons baking powder
225 g/8 oz flour

For the syrup
225 g/8 oz sugar
150 ml/¼ pint water
2 teaspoons orange flower water *or* rosewater

100 g/4 oz whipped cream or crème fraîche, to decorate

Lightly grease a Swiss roll tin. Beat the cottage cheese with the buttermilk, eggs, melted butter and sugar. Sift the baking powder and flour together and beat this mixture into the cake mixture. Turn the mixture into the tin and bake it in a preheated moderately hot oven (190°C, 375°F, Gas 5) oven for 30 minutes.

Meanwhile, put the sugar and water into a heavy-based pan. Bring to the boil without stirring, brushing down any crystals that form on the inside of the pan. Boil rapidly for 10 minutes. Remove from the heat and add the orange flower water or rosewater. Pour the syrup over the cake while it is still warm. Eat it soon after making, with the whipped cream or crème fraîche, preferably while the cake is still warm.

MELOPITTA
Serves 12

This is another Greek cheese pie of very ancient origin. Unsalted mizithra (anari) cheese should be used. If it is not available, use ricotta or other low-fat soft cheese.

225 g/8 oz flour
225 g/8 oz butter
450 g/1 lb low-fat soft cheese, at room
    temperature
100 g/4 oz honey
75 g/3 oz brown sugar
4 eggs
2 teaspoons ground cinnamon

Grease two 23-cm/9-inch pie dishes. Sift the flour into a bowl. Cut the butter into small pieces and rub it into the flour, until the mixture resembles bread crumbs. Add about 3 tablespoons of water, just enough to make the mixture cohere into a firm dough. Knead the dough briefly, then wrap it in cling film and leave it in the refrigerator for 30 minutes.

Roll out the dough as thinly as possible and use it to line the two pie dishes. Beat the cheese with an electric mixer until it is light and fluffy. Beat in the honey and brown sugar, then the eggs one at a time. When the mixture is smooth, divide it between the two pie dishes and sprinkle each with half a teaspoon of cinnamon. Bake the pie in a preheated moderately hot oven (190°C, 375°F, Gas 5) for 35 minutes. Remove from the oven and sprinkle each pie with the rest of the cinnamon. Serve chilled.

CREAM CHEESE BUNS
(Koláčy)
Makes 12

These delicious buns come from Czechoslovakia. They are best eaten as soon as possible after baking. When using yeast, keep all ingredients warm and rinse all utensils in hot water (dry them thoroughly) immediately before use. If using dried yeast, follow the manufacturer's instructions. Some yeasts must be mixed with the dry ingredients first, in which case add the yeast to the bowl with the flour and salt.

For the buns
25 g/1 oz fresh yeast *or* 15 g/½ oz dried yeast
150 ml/¼ pint lukewarm water
1 teaspoon sugar
225 g/8 oz strong plain flour
¼ teaspoon salt
150 g/5 oz butter
1 egg, beaten

For the filling
225 g/8 oz full-fat soft cheese
1 small egg
1 tablespoon sugar
¼ teaspoon vanilla essence
1 teaspoon grated lemon rind
25 g/1 oz sultanas

To make the buns, dissolve the yeast in the water in a small bowl. Add half the sugar, cover with cling film and leave in a warm place for 20 minutes or until it is foaming. Sift the flour and salt into a bowl. Rub in 25 g/1 oz of the butter. Add the yeast mixture and the egg. Combine the ingredients into a firm dough. Turn the dough onto a floured board and knead it until it is elastic and does not stick to your fingers, about 10 minutes.

Roll out the dough into a rectangle, about 1-cm/½-inch thick. Cut the rest of the butter into small pieces and cover two-thirds of the rectangle with them. Fold the unbuttered third inwards over the buttered third, and fold the last buttered third on top. Press the edges to seal in the butter and roll out the dough into a rectangle again. Give the dough a quarter turn and repeat the folding process, though without adding any butter. Roll out again. Give the dough another quarter turn and roll it out again. Fold it as before, and wrap it in cling film. Refrigerate the dough for 1 hour.

To make the filling, beat all the ingredients except the sultanas until smooth. Stir in the sultanas, making sure they are distributed evenly throughout. Roll out the dough to a rectangle 30-cm/12-inches by-23-cm/9-inches and cut it into 7-cm/3-inch squares. Place 2 teaspoons of filling in the centre of each square. Fold the corners of each square towards the centre, to enclose the filling. Let the buns rise on a greased baking tray in a warm place for 1 hour or until well-risen.

Bake the buns in a preheated hot oven (230°C, 450°F, Gas 8) for 15 minutes, or until lightly browned. The buns will keep for up to 1 week and freeze well. If they are frozen, reheat before serving.

ITALIAN EASTER TARTS
Makes 24

These delicate little tartlets are eaten in Northern Italy and are known as *Pastiera di Pasqua*.

For the pastry dough
100 g/4 oz butter
100 g/4 oz flour
50 g/2 oz sugar
2 teaspoons lemon juice
1 egg yolk
50 g/2 oz ground almonds
½ teaspoon ground cinnamon

For the filling
75 g/3 oz pearl tapioca, soaked in water overnight
300 ml/½ pint milk
½ teaspoon grated lemon rind
150 g/5 oz caster sugar
salt
225 g/½ lb cream cheese
1 egg, separated
50 g/2 oz mixed peel, chopped
½ teaspoon ground cinnamon

To make the dough, cut the butter into small pieces and rub it into the flour, until the mixture resembles bread crumbs. Add the sugar, lemon juice, egg yolk, almonds and cinnamon. Mix well, adding a couple of tablespoons of cold water if necessary, to make a fairly stiff dough. Wrap the dough in cling film and refrigerate it for at least 30 minutes.

Reserve one quarter of the dough. Roll out the rest until it is 5 mm/¼ inch thick and use it to line greased tartlet tins. Prick the bottoms of the pastry and bake "blind" in a preheated moderately hot oven (190°C, 375°F, Gas 5) for 5 minutes.

Drain the tapioca and add to it the milk, lemon rind, 25 g/1 oz of the sugar and a pinch of salt. Cover the pan and simmer about 15 minutes or until all the milk has been absorbed.

Beat together the cream cheese and the remaining sugar and beat in the egg yolk. Beat in the cooked tapioca, then the peel and cinnamon. Whisk the egg white into stiff peaks and fold it into the mixture. Fill the tartlets two-thirds full with the mixture. Roll out the reserved dough and slice it into strips about 5 mm/¼ inch wide. Arrange two strips in a cross on each of the tarts. Bake in a preheated moderately hot oven (190°C, 375°F, Gas 5) for 15 minutes. Cool on wire racks.

SWEET CHEESE CRESCENTS
Makes 24

Like so many crescent-shaped cakes and breads, this is another Austrian speciality. Since the crescent was the Turkish symbol, a never-ending stream of crescent-shaped goodies was created after the Turks were defeated at the gates of Vienna in 1683.

For the dough
225 g/8 oz flour
½ teaspoon salt
225 g/8 oz butter, chilled
225 g/8 oz full-fat soft cheese, chilled
100 g/4 oz icing sugar

For the filling
100 g/4 oz walnuts, chopped
50 g/2 oz seedless raisins, chopped
100 g/4 oz sugar
2 teaspoons ground cinnamon

Sift the flour and salt into a bowl. Chop the butter and cream cheese into small pieces and cut them into the flour with a pastry cutter or fork, until the mixture resembles bread crumbs. Work the dough into a ball. Wrap it in cling film and refrigerate it for at least 1 hour.

Divide the dough into three equal pieces. Leave two pieces in the refrigerator. Roll out the remaining piece between two sheets of floured greaseproof paper into a 23-cm/9-inch circle. Cut the circle into eight equal wedges.

Combine all the filling ingredients in the order given. Place a teaspoon of filling on each wedge and roll it up, starting at the wide end. Curve the biscuits into a crescent shape. Sift the icing sugar into a bowl and thoroughly coat each crescent. Place on baking trays. Repeat with the other two-thirds of the dough.

Bake the crescents in a preheated moderately hot oven (200°C, 400°F, Gas 6) for 25 minutes. Sprinkle with more icing sugar before serving.

CHEESECAKES WITHOUT CHEESE

This may seem an extraordinary idea for a book on cheesecakes! However, when looking through old cookbooks, one often comes across recipes labelled "cheesecake," which contain no cheese whatsoever. These recipes are of two types: they either contain a custard or junket mixture of the consistency of a cream cheese, or they contain a fruit cheese, such as damson cheese or lemon curd. It should be remembered that before refrigeration was commonplace, there was no way of preserving unmatured cheeses. Cheese for cheesecakes had to be made from the freshest new milk, soured so that it separated into curds and whey. The curdling agent was usually rennet, made from the stomach of a ruminant; however, herbs such as Lady's Bedstraw have also been used to sour cheese. In fact, the product sold in health food shops as "vegetarian cheese," is cheese that is made with a vegetable curdling agent. Only in parts of the country where large amounts of curd cheese were made at a certain time of the year (usually Whitsun) could curd cheese be bought ready made. So cakes were devised that tasted like cheesecakes but contained no cheese.

Vegetarian cheesecakes are also included here for people who are allergic to cow's milk. Tofu, now commonly available in health food shops and good supermarkets, is just as suitable for sweet dishes as for savoury ones. It makes mouthwatering cheesecakes, if they are strongly flavoured with other ingredients, since the tofu itself is virtually tasteless. This is a wonderful serving idea for dinner guests who don't or can't eat dairy products.

VICTORIAN RICE CHEESECAKES
Makes 24 tartlets

This is one version of the cheeseless cheesecake. It is a rich and delicious mixture. If you do not like to use brandy, use brandy flavouring.

1 quantity Tartlet Pastry (see page 54)
50 g/2 oz long-grained rice
150 ml/¼ pint whipping cream
100 g/4 oz unsalted butter
100 g/4 oz sugar
1 tablespoon orange flower water
1 teaspoon grated lemon rind
3 eggs, beaten
2 tablespoons brandy

Roll out the Tartlet Pastry (see page 54) and cut it with a pastry cutter to fit two greased 12-cup tartlet tins. Line the tins with the dough. Bake the pastry in a preheated moderate oven (180°C, 350°F, Gas 4) for 15 minutes.

Bring a pan containing 1 litre/2 pints water to the boil. Add the rice, cover the pan and simmer until tender, about 20 minutes. Drain the rice and rinse it under the cold tap. Put it into a saucepan with the cream, butter, sugar, orange flower water and grated lemon rind. Beat it well until smooth, then stir in the beaten eggs and brandy. Cook, stirring, over low heat until the mixture thickens, but do not let it boil or it will curdle. Remove from the heat and let it cool. Fill the tartlets three-quarters full with the mixture and bake them in a preheated moderate oven (180°C, 350°F, Gas 4) for 15 minutes or until the tops are golden brown.

TOFU CHEESECAKE
Serves 12

Once you have tried using tofu to make a cheesecake, you may never go back to real cheese again! Tofu is fermented bean curd, just as cheese is fermented milk. You can find it in any health food store and in good supermarkets. It needs draining before use, and sometimes it should be drained while being weighted down. The techniques for making tofu "cheese-cakes" are almost identical to those for baked cheesecakes. However, since tofu is more fragile, and therefore liable to crack, the cakes should be transferred directly from the oven to the refrigerator.

For the base
225 g/8 oz digestive biscuits, crushed
75 g/3 oz butter, melted
1 teaspoon ground cinnamon

For the filling
900 g/2 lb tofu
3 tablespoons lemon juice
1 tablespoon vanilla essence
½ teaspoon salt
6 tablespoons salad oil
6 tablespoons honey
225 g/8 oz sugar

Decoration
2 kiwi fruit, peeled and sliced
75 g/3 oz seedless black grapes, halved

Mix the ingredients for the base together. Press them into the base and up the sides of an ungreased 23-cm/9-inch springform tin. Chill until required. Combine the filling ingredients in the order given. Pour them into the prepared crust and bake in a preheated moderately hot oven (190°C, 375°F, Gas 5) for 40 minutes, or until firm. Turn off the heat and cool the cake in the oven for 30 minutes, then chill immediately. Serve well chilled, decorated with sliced kiwi fruit and black grapes.

INDEX